AURICULAS
THROUGH THE AGES
Bear's Ears, Ricklers and Painted Ladies

AURICULAS
THROUGH THE AGES

Bear's Ears, Ricklers and Painted Ladies

PATRICIA CLEVELAND-PECK
ILLUSTRATED BY ELISABETH DOWLE

THE CROWOOD PRESS

First published in 2011 by
The Crowood Press Ltd
Ramsbury, Marlborough
Wiltshire SN8 2HR

www.crowood.com

British Library Cataloguing-in-Publication Data
A catalogue record for this book is available from the British Library.

ISBN 978 1 84797 249 1

Frontispiece: The portrait of Martha Rodes by Christopher Steele painted in 1750
marks an important moment in the history of the auricula, the advent of the edged
flower.

To Dennis and Justin
for their unstinting support with all my auricula projects

Typeset by Servis Filmsetting Ltd, Stockport, Cheshire
Printed and bound in India by Replika Press Pvt Ltd

Contents

List of Plates

Preface

On the day I reached the top of the Kitzbüheler Horn high in the Austrian Alps the sun was shining but the air was fresh with the memory of snow. From my perch two thousand metres up however, it was not the magnificent view but the masses of yellow *Primula auricula* growing on the rocky outcrops at my feet that absorbed me. For these simple flowers with their greyish leaves and umbrels of butter-yellow flowers nodding in the breeze are the ancestor plants of today's exquisite auricula cultivars that growers have refined for us to enjoy today.

In tracing the history of this flower there could be no better place to begin. In the words of the great auricula enthusiast, the Rev. C. Oscar Moreton (1888–1977), founder and past president, Southern Section of the National Primula and Auricula Society: 'Of all the many thousands of wild auriculas which grow among the Alps the greater part are never seen by the eye of man. ...To see such a plant for the first time, growing in its native place in the rocky turf of a steep Alpine mountainside, is an experience not easily forgotten, and leaves something of its glory imprinted on the mind.'

In following the story of this plant from its Alpine origins, I have endeavoured to set it within its social and historical context and to single out some of the interesting men and women who have felt passionate about it. The auricula has counted amongst its admirers herbalists, scholars, duchesses, kings, clergymen, weavers and miners, before levelling out in today's world to be admired by anyone who appreciates things of beauty. One such lover of beauty was the poet and critic Sacheverell Sitwell (1897–1988).

When my very first auricula bloomed and I saw the truss of grey-edged pips shimmering with farina above silvery leaves, it had about it such an air of artificiality that I had to touch it to make sure that it was real. That is what is so special about this plant.

Flowers have always carried messages, and throughout its history the little auricula has had a lot to say for itself. 'I am beautiful, and you who have perfected me are cultured' is what it whispered to the eighteenth-century florist. 'No member of the gentry can do better than you', it reassured the weaver as he took the first prize at the Florists' Feast. 'Keep going, I can surprise you yet' is its challenge to today's hybridists.

Of course I did not immediately realize what a wealth of social, political, economic, religious, intellectual, economic and aesthetic history this little plant embodies. If, I reflected, flowers stand where nature and culture meet, this must be the very point of convergence.

The perfection of this flower has been achieved by the human hands of patient florists – today's hybridizers – over several centuries. They delighted in the minutiae of the plant and strove to breed ever-improved varieties, developing the refined plants that we give our rigorous scrutiny, and in turn give us intense pleasure.

This plant is not just a living thing but a living antique. Gazing at its elegance of form, I saw for myself what Sitwell meant when he wrote, 'there is no flower so evocative of the past as the auricula'.

Elisabeth and I both have our own collections of auriculas, but we are not hybridists nor do we exhibit our plants, although we deeply respect the work of the people who do. We care for our plants, delight in their flowering and enjoy displaying them, but I fear we are just the sort of 'country-women' Samuel Gilbert was referring to in 1682, and that our beloved auriculas are simply the 'trifles' which he considered 'of no esteem to a Florist who is taken up with things of more value'.

This book arose from our chance meeting in a local nursery. At the time I did not know that Elisabeth Dowle was a well-known botanical artist, and she did not know I was a garden writer. That became apparent as we became friends and decided to collaborate on this project.

We were motivated by the fact that all the available books are illustrated by photographs, and to quote Sacheverell Sitwell again, 'Mere photographs of the Auricula convey nothing whatever of its qualities: these can only be translated through the hand of an artist and it is a flower that is technically difficult to capture on paper'. Elisabeth has captured it definitively in this series of watercolours, which we hope will not only give the reader pleasure but also provide a record of some of the superb auriculas available now, in the twenty-first century.

The story sets out to tell how these simple species plants living high in the Alpine regions hybridized and made their way down into the gardens of Europe and out into the world. It tells how they were named and classified by herbalists before the meticulous work of florists transformed them into the living jewels we see depicted here – small treasures which are within the reach of us all.

We hope that you will enjoy accompanying us on this journey.

ACKNOWLEDGMENTS

Firstly I should like to express gratitude to The Authors' Foundation without whose grant I should have been unable to research this book. Next I should like to thank Elisabeth Dowle who invited me to collaborate with her on the project.

I am grateful to the present-day florists who have contributed to the Appendix. Many other people, private individuals and staff of libraries and institutions have answered my queries with patience and kindness. Especial thanks go to Dr Stephen Harris, Dr David Leith, Dr Libing Zang, Dr Susy Marcon, Derek Parsons, David Tarver and my three 'library angels', Florike Egmont, Sylvia van Zanen and Esther van Gelder of The Clusius Project Leiden.

I am also grateful to Ben Groen, Dr Mark Spenser, Dr Charlie Jarvis, Dr Georg Gärtner, Dr John Richards, Dr Frank Taylor, Eva Hofer, Ina ten Hove-Janesma, Andrea Hart, Heidi Hermann, Jeanne and Florence Monier, Celia Dixie, Allan Guest, Dr Dennis Baker, Ken Saint, Paula Finden, Lucia Tomasi Tongiorgi, Anna Pavord, Alice Lemaire, Lawrence Wigley, Brigitte Wachsmuth, Geoff Nicholle, Kate Gwillym, Gerard Thijsse, Hanne Kolind-Paulsen, Catherine Stevenson, Claude Jourde, Silvia Scott, Anne Townsend, Kerry Webb, Saskia Helin, Louise Mould, and the staff of the Lindley Library, especially Liz Gilbert and Elizabeth Koper.

Finally my gratitude goes to my family, who probably never want to hear the word auricula again.

Snooty Fox.

Illustrator's Preface

Throughout the years spent painting these auriculas, my initial fascination with the genus has grown, and I hope that in attempting to evoke their beauty I have managed to convey how enchanting these little plants are, with their diverse form and extraordinary colour range.

It has never been my intention to depict perfect prizewinning specimens. Instead I have tried to capture the character of each variety in a realistic manner as it grows, sometimes with multiple stems and the occasional misshapen pip or untidy growing habit resulting from variable climate and soil conditions. However, despite these apparent flaws, each plant has its own charm, which transcends strict showbench stipulations, and I felt was worthy of inclusion.

In certain varieties, there appears to be a degree of variation in form, size and colour in plants obtained from different nurseries, so it has not always been a straightforward matter to establish exactly what is considered typical.

With so many hundreds of named varieties, it is also inevitable that the occasional mislabelling occurs, albeit inadvertently. Many of the auriculas I have painted were those from specialist nurseries that caught my eye. Some have been given to me by growers, and others the author and I grew ourselves. Several were acquired from the late Brenda Hyatt, who went on to verify my drawings, and offered advice and guidance regarding which varieties to paint.

Elisabeth Dowle
www.elisabethdowle.com

ACKNOWLEDGEMENTS

I should like to thank Robin and Annabel Graham of Drointon Nurseries, whose superb packing meant that plants arrived in perfect condition. Also Derek Parsons whose advice and generosity regarding striped varieties was invaluable.

I am especially grateful to Clare Clements who was instrumental in starting this book. She also provided me with the first plants for my ever-increasing collection of auriculas, which continue to be a source of great pleasure and joy.

Lastly thank you to John for his patience, building endless shelters for my plants, and to Mat for his technical help.

CHAPTER 1

Categories

Throughout this book I make use of the umbrella term 'auricula', but as today we are blessed with more and better cultivars than earlier enthusiasts could have imagined, in this chapter I shall, with the help of Elisabeth's images, attempt to untangle some of the complexities of the categories used today to differentiate them.

In the book that first transported me to the world of auriculas, the 1939 volume *Old Fashioned Flowers*, the poet and art critic Sacheverell Sitwell (1897–1988) refers with deep admiration to the Stage Auricula, which we sometimes find called the Florists' Auricula. 'There is no flower so immediately irresistible as the Auricula. The first moment of seeing a Stage Auricula is an experience never to be forgotten ... for the perfection of a Stage Auricula is that of the most exquisite Meissen porcelain, or the most lovely silk stuffs of Isfahan ... and yet it is a living and growing thing.'

We sometimes find it called the Florists' Auricula, as in Sir Rowland Biffen's excellently informative 1949 book *The Auricula*. Biffen (1874–1949) was a brilliant Cambridge botanist and geneticist who contributed enormously to our understanding of this plant.

It would seem that Sitwell was entranced by what we would call Show Auriculas, while Biffen used the term to designate auriculas of a superior quality that could be exhibited.

Here I have restricted myself to discussing the basics of each type, but a plant of exhibition quality must posses other qualities: size, shape, symmetry, proportion together with other more arbitrary requirements, detail of which can be found in the guides of each of the three National Auricula and Primula Societies.

SHOW AURICULAS

Show Auriculas are the aristocrats of the auricula world. They are characterized by a dense ring of farina, a white powdery substance, around the eye of the flower. In some auriculas farina dusts the leaves as well as the eye, and it can also pattern the reverse of the petals in a most attractive way. The fact that this farina can be washed away by rain is one of the reasons that Show Auriculas are grown in pots and kept under cover.

Also known as meal or paste, farina is such a unique and important feature of the auricula, and one that adds so greatly to its beauty, that it requires some explanation. Farina resembles a fine white powder, but it is in fact an unusual type of glandular hair. If looked at under a microscope each hair is seen to be a transparent globe carried on a short stalk composed of smaller cells through which protrude large numbers of fine filaments of a waxy nature. The whole structure, as Biffen so graphically put it, 'has the appearance of a short handled household mop'. The hairs are massed together and form a uniform white layer which, to an insect walking over it, would have 'a soft rough surface on which footprints show up like those of a rabbit on snow.' According to Derek Parsons, one of today's leading hybridizers, there are two sorts of farina, the opaque floury sort and a finer more crystalline type through which the tissue of the plant beneath remains visible.

Show Auriculas are further divided into Edges and Selfs.

Facing page: Oban.

Edges

If Shows are the aristocrats of the auricula world, then the Edges are the royal family. They were first noticed in the eighteenth century and occur as a result of a mutation by which the edges of the petals became leaf-like.

Green-edged flowers are those where this leaf tissue does not have any paste or farina on it, but remains green.

Grey-edged flowers have a dusting of paste.

White-edged flowers have a thick coating of paste. Between the ring of paste and the edge, there is a thin irregular band of colour known as the ground colour. Until recently the requirement was that this should be black, but now any other colour is acceptable provided 'it is bright, rich, unshaded and free from meal'.

Fancies may be classed as plants that do not conform to the basic standards but are sufficiently striking to make them worth retaining. Many are edged plants that have a ground, or body, colour other than black but lack the necessary form and proportion to be classed as Show Auriculas. It is from this loose category that new breaks can occur.

Selfs have the circle of farina, but the petals (which can be yellow, red, blue, dark and any other colour) are of an even colour with no shading and no edge.

Until the early twentieth century Shows were the only type of auricula to be found on the show bench. Now all the categories have their classes.

ALPINE AURICULAS

These were originally known as 'Shaded Selfs' and were distinguished from other Shows by the absence of farina. Their leaves should not bear any meal, and their petals should be large. Another key characteristic is that the petals should shade from darker near the centre to lighter near the edge. Alpines are really no less beautiful than Shows, and their velvety petals come in a wide range of sumptuous, rich and jewel-like colours.

Alpines are in turn subdivided into Gold Centred and Light Centred.

Gold centred are those with a yellow or gold ground surrounding the central tube (which contains the reproductive organs) and petals in the gold, brown, orange and red tones.

Light centred are those with a white or cream centre and petals in the blue, purple, mauve and red tones. A difference in the acidity of the cell sap in the tissue accounts for the colour variations.

DOUBLES

Once widely grown and very fashionable, Doubles were neglected for many years but have now made a remarkable comeback. As Allan Guest writes in his 2009 book *The Auricula*, 'In this group the breeders and their efforts must take the greatest praise for they have raised what was once a group of ragamuffins … to the level of beauty, of form and grace which would often be the equal of jewellery or plasterwork fit to grace any stately home.'

The colour range is wide, and meal may be present either as paste or stripes.

STRIPES

Biffen writing in 1949 commented, 'The Striped or Flaked Auriculas are a group which has been long since disappeared from cultivation'. Now thanks to the work of such devoted hybridizers as the late Alan Hawkes and Derek Parsons we have an array of striking plants which would have delighted the florists of the eighteenth century. The stripes should be even and well defined.

BORDER AURICULAS

Border or Garden Auriculas are the least developed type. They are considered by some to be the poor relations of the tribe and have been referred to as the 'mongrels' or 'the rag-bag' of auriculas. Some are reminiscent of the wild *Primula auricula*, but the forms and sizes are extremely varied; some have frilled petals and some rounded; some bear farina while others do not. Many of the plants however are not only beautiful in their own right but also sweetly scented. Generally speaking they are quite happy in the open garden.

The auricula is extremely unusual plant in that it holds within its gene pool such an enormous variety of forms and colours. Sitwell rather charmingly compares this to 'the many and varying ingredients of lyric poetry which are mixed in every generation in new proportions'.

All categories of auriculas are in fact part of a larger continuum, and the accepted classes detailed above are only the segments of this spectrum which have been picked out and specified by florists as desirable. They are thus man-made constructs or ideals envisaged by man, which have been imposed on the developing plants according to the dictates of prevailing taste and fashion.

Different choices could have been selected and the categories would then have been quite different from those we have today. The Rev. Francis Daltry Horner (1837–1912), an auricula enthusiast and writer commented in 1877 that had the florist not considered the accepted standards, 'we might have a starfish form, a flower of narrow windmill petals instead of one fair disc ... we might have misdirected the Picotee into a fantastic fimbriate flower, as fringy in its way as those frilled paper anklet that set off festive legs of ham'.

The genetic potential of this continuum is such that it throws up all sorts of variations from which the florist, by careful selection, chooses from the seedlings the ones that meet the accepted ideal of consummate beauty – the Standards of Excellence of the day – and reject the rest. The potential is by no means exhausted and although our present auriculas are of a quality never before seen, as we shall see, the story has not yet ended.

Pioneer Stripe.

Facing page: Hinton Fields.

CHAPTER 2

How the Auricula Got Its Name

This book concerns the history and development of today's auricula, of which thousands of magnificent cultivars are now available in commerce. The plant is descended from wild species plants, one of which, somewhat confusingly, is also called *Primula auricula*. So how did this plant originate?

Long before they were formally classed as primulas, the ancestors of the plants we know as auriculas had for centuries been growing high in the mountainous areas of Europe; in the Pyrenees, Alps and Dolomites. They had probably been crushed underfoot by Roman legions crossing the Alps and had been gathered by local folk throughout the Middle Ages.

At this period they would of course have had common names that changed not only from country to country but from valley to valley. These names in turn would have altered over the years. Thus, as a preliminary to following the development of the auricula from its alpine origins, I want to follow the changes through which the name passed as efforts to observe, classify and communicate became more important.

Amongst human beings, as soon as something is found or made there has always been a need to give it a name in order to talk about it to other people. So throughout history when a plant was discovered the name allocated to it was often connected with its use or appearance. Many of these common names still hold within them these shadowy and often poetic evocations of the past. These names could, however, only be employed amongst people who recognized them, and were thus restricted to quite small areas, as even a few miles away a common name could refer to a completely different plant. There are, for example, some ninety different common names in English for *Caltha palustris*, the Marsh Marigold and almost as many for *Cardamine pratensis*, Lady's Smock.

Thus, in order to communicate across boundaries it became increasingly important to standardize names. This happened to our potential auricula when herbalists began to talk to each other about it, and the name heard most frequently throughout Europe, although even this degree of standardization did not become widespread until the sixteenth century, was *Auricula ursi*. Translated, this became Bear's Ears in English, *Oreilles d'Ours* in French, *Orrechia d'Orso* in Italian, *Oreja de Orso* in Spanish, *Bärenöhrlein* in German and *Beeren Oor* in Dutch. There are several theories, none particularly evident, as to why this name was selected: the furriness of some of the leaves, the leaf shape or the little pedicle which it sometimes grows and which can flop over and so resemble a bear's ear. *Auricula ursi* was, however, the name which botanists gave our auricula's forebears for many years.

Attempts to classify plants began with the ancients who saw natural history, including plants, as a branch of philosophy, the stuff of wisdom and knowledge. Aristotle wrote a book on animals which inspired his pupil Theophrastus (*c*.372–287BC) to write one of the first important books on plants. Theophrastus in fact was known as 'The Father of Botany' (although botany as a science had not then been named) and in his book he recorded some 500 types of plant.

Facing page: George Swinford's Leathercoat.

THE MEDICAL CONNECTION

The most influential of the ancient plant writers and one whose name continued to resound down the centuries was Dioscorides, who also lived in the first century AD. He studied in Alexandria, became a *medicus legionis* in the Roman army, travelling with troops, gathering and preparing herbs for their injuries. In his *De Materia Medica,* he named some 600 medicinal plants including drugs such as cannabis and the opium poppy, although in some cases he attached the wrong names to the plants. Nevertheless his advice to herbalists to study plants and learn their characteristics and to 'be present when the plants shoot out of the earth, when they are fully grown and when they begin to fade' established an important principle. Most of the plants he mentioned had, like the ancestors of the auricula, been growing for centuries, known to local people who foraged for them, ate them and used them as cures. Plants then were regarded very differently from nowadays. Not only were they valued mainly for utilitarian reasons but often in ways which strike us as extremely strange. Dioscorides, for example, believed that asparagus grew from ram's horns and would, if hung around the neck, cause barrenness.

Herbalists

The Hippocratic theory known as 'the humours' claimed that the body consists of the fluids of phlegm, blood, yellow bile and black bile. Each of these possessed a certain characteristic, being hot, wet, dry, or cold, and it was believed that good health depended on a balance between them. This was even relevant to foodstuffs. John Parkinson (1567–1650) author of *Paradisi in sole paradises terrestris,* one of the finest herbals in the English language, refers to his love of 'hot' herbs like thyme, hyssop and penny royal. Even as late as 1699, the eminently sensible gardener and diarist John Evelyn (1620–1706) in his book on salads, *Acetaria,* sometimes categorizes his salad ingredients as hot, cold, wet or dry – a reference not so much to their taste or texture but to their efficacy according to this classical doctrine of humours.

Even more important to early herbalists was the principle that plants were there for the use of man, and if the use of a plant was not known, then it was waiting to be discovered. The whole point of the early herbals was to indicate the 'virtues' or pharmaceutical benefits of each plant. Paracelsus (1493–1541) even considered that man knew intuitively which plants could serve him, and Giambattista della Porta (1535–1615), a fervent searcher after the 'secrets of nature' in his *Phytognomica,* went so far as to say that the locality of a plant could likewise be an indication of its use – willow for example, growing in wet places, would be good for rheumatism which is caused by damp. This, in fact, was echoed in German-speaking areas, where the fledgling auricula was known as *swindelkraut* – or 'giddiness plant' – on the principle that as it grew in the high mountains it would, in the words of one of England's best known herbalists John Gerard (1542–1612), be useful for 'strengthening the head when on top of places which are high, so giddiness and swimming of the braine may not affect them'.

Nowadays the benefits of herbal medicine are being rediscovered. A resurgence of interest in folk 'cures' has resulted in extensive quests to discover or rediscover beneficial plants. The adage that 'plants can live without man but man cannot live without plants' is as true now as it ever was.

Not quite so obvious is the idea held in the past that efficacy of the plant was revealed to the physician through the 'Doctrine of Signatures', a system whereby the use of a plant was supposedly indicated by its appearance. A walnut, resembling the human brain, was considered to be useful for head troubles, and the spotted leaves of the pulmonaria, or lungwort, were thought to cure respiratory diseases. Although it now seems rather naive, it could be argued that even this system did contribute towards the rationalization of names.

For medical purposes it was obviously extremely important that plants were correctly identified. Selection of the wrong type could – and did – result in fatalities. This was illustrated by the controversy that raged in London in the sixteenth

Facing page: Walton.

century over the popular imported cure-all known as 'Venice Treacle', which was used for everything from toothache to running sores. The main constituent was a sea onion or squill, *Scilla alba*, but the problem arose when British apothecaries began to make the treacle themselves, sometimes incorporating another type of sea onion, the red squill, which was such a 'strong and potent poison' that when in Spain, the great botanist Charles de l'Ecluse (1526–1609) was warned against even touching it.

Apothecaries

Apothecaries with their ready access to poisons were always suspect. The great John Parkinson was himself in 1595 summonsed to go before the committee of the College of Physicians to answer a complaint 'of having extorted money from a woman who charged him even with the homicide of her husband'. In fact the charge was nothing to do with the homicide but was brought against Parkinson for 'practising' as a doctor. In this case Parkinson got off as he was able to impress the committee with his knowledge, but apothecaries were not doctors, and their practising without a licence could result in time spent in prison.

It is hardly surprising that physicians and apothecaries were regarded with suspicion, as they literally held the power of life and death in their hands. In England the divisions between what the university-educated physicians and the apprenticed apothecaries and barber surgeons (who drew teeth and let blood) were permitted to do were more strictly observed than on the continent. Physicians, however, were expensive, so for people with access to a still room where perfumes and herbal tinctures for medicinal use were distilled, that would be their first port of all, the second being a 'wise woman' down the road, and the third a visit to the apothecary's shop, after which there was nothing but to let the illness run its course.

Simple Gatherers

In most cases the medicinal plants or 'simples' as they were known, were collected by country people, often 'wise women', who knew exactly where to find the best specimens in their locality, knowledge which they guarded very closely. They were not looked upon with great favour by those higher up the chain, and in the early herbals there are plenty of examples of derogatory remarks about old women and rustics.

Nevertheless some botanists did give the herb women credit for their knowledge. Otto Brunfels (1488–1534) who learnt from a country woman that the herb Good King Henry was a pot herb, tells the story of a dinner party for members of the Paris Faculty of Medicine given by a physician-humanist during which the host pulled a herb out of a green salad and asked the guest if they knew its name. None did, and they concluded that it must be something very rare and exotic. The kitchen maid was summoned – and told them it was parsley.

Some of the procedures used then were arcane and involved magical and semi-religious rituals. These were still the days when the alchemist's goal of using magical astrological symbols to synthesize gold from base metals was being pursued. The power of the plant was thought to be influenced by the phases of the moon; to dig some types up with an iron tool was said to leach away their virtues while other methods were so mysterious that they were nearer spells than cures.

At the time however, although correct identification was an essential, the herbals contained many errors that increased each time they were copied (the text of Dioscorides for example, went through numerous editions over ten centuries). If one also considers that many of the original writers (and some of the illustrators) had never seen the living plant but based their descriptions on previous works, it is not surprising that mistakes were made – mistakes that increased considerably with the influx of exotic plant material from the New World.

THE BOTANISTS

Gesner

So what of the predecessors of our auricula, the *Auricula ursi*? I have found unsubstantiated references to this name's being used in the late fifteenth century, but it was certainly used by the great Conrad Gesner (1515–1556) in his posthumously published *Historia Plantarum*, which was written in the last ten years of his life. He also includes a helpful illustration which will be discussed in due course. Gesner, a genius with a gift for collating and organizing facts, lived most of his life in Zurich. He was a devotee of the mountains and their alpine flora – it was his habit to climb at least one mountain a year, not only to collect flowers but also for his health. He is remembered mainly as a zoologist (and the inventor of the pencil) and it is a pity that he died from the plague before seeing his great work on plants published.

Mattiolus

A writer who lived to see his work not only published but also become the best selling herbal ever produced was the famous Sienese botanist and physician Pier Andrea Mattioli or Mattiolus (1501–77), who spent twenty years in Prague in the service of Emperor Ferdinand I. Mattiolus used the term *Auricula ursi* in his version of Dioscorides' *De Materia Medica*. In common with many of the early botanists, he had a network of correspondents who sent him comments which he incorporated into the work. For the six-book outcome, *Commentarii in sex libros Pedacii Dioscoridis,* he took Dioscorides' text and annotated, adapted and updated it. Published in Venice in 1544, it went into over sixty editions and sold a phenomenal 32,000 copies in Mattoilus's lifetime.

Regarding auriculas, we find an entry for *Auricula ursi* amongst the *Saniculae*. It is illustrated by a woodcut which shows a plant quite similar to a simple border auricula. It has thick leaves and roots and bears on its stalk a truss of about a dozen pips (individual blooms), some in bud, some with five open petals. The entry is not long, and Mattiolus followed the set formula used by herbalists: the plant would be described; the place or places where it had been found would be mentioned; there would be a section on its 'virtues' or benefits, and the synonyms or other names associated with the plant used by previous herbalists would be listed. These synonyms can be confusing as some of the names would seem to belong to

quite different plants. One of the most common of the additional names found in association with *Auricula ursi* is, as here, *Sanicula* (which implies healing qualities) and *alpina* from its mountain birthplace.

Mattiolus preferred to leave the plant collecting to others, so we cannot be sure that he ever handled the plant, but in general his attempts at identification were more accurate than most of the other commentators, so when he included this *Auricula ursi* it seems very likely that it is the ancestor of our auricula.

Michiel

Woodblocks had been used to depict plants in herbals from the end of the fifteenth century, but they often resulted in somewhat crude images. A contemporary of Mattiolus, the Venetian, Pietro Antonio Michiel (1510–76) offers us better clues to the auricula's provenance by including in his book the first illustrations painted in colour. Three images are found in *Cinque Libri di Piante*, which is composed of five books: the blue, the yellow, the green and the two red books.

During the 1540s botanical gardens were established at Pisa, Padua and Florence. The Padua botanical garden, which belonged to the wealthy Senate of the Venetian Republic, benefited from the many exotic species brought from other parts of the world by the seafaring Venetians. This influx of strange new plants gave a great impetus to interest in botany, as the Venetians were not slow to see the economic value of new herbs and rare spices.

These were very exciting days for botanists. Michiel, a nobleman with a great interest in and knowledge of plants, was a member of the important network of botanists working at the beginning of the sixteenth century in Italy. This group also included Mattiolus, as well as Luca Ghini (1490–1556) who set up the botanic garden at Pisa, and his pupil Ulisse Aldrovandi (1522–1605) who became curator of the Bologna botanic garden, founded later in 1568. They corresponded and exchanged plants, seeds and information.

Michiel was particularly interested in the systemization of plants, and while planning his book he compared names and forms with Aldrovandi,

Grey Monarch.

who had a more hands-on approach than many other scholars. Aldrovandi claimed he described only those things that he had 'seen with my own eyes, touched with my hands, dissected, and likewise observed one by one in my little world of nature'. Michiel had a similar practical approach and believed in learning as much as possible from the acclimatization and cultivation of plants as he did from a theoretical approach.

In a letter to Aldrovandi dated 10 April 1554 he wrote, 'It is not possible to do great things with a little sprig of dried plant material, you need an effort like mine ... I have suffered a lot in growing my plants, nourishing them and seeing them from beginning to end – it is then we find all their qualities, so that the painter with his brush and I with my pen can extract from them all the information possible'. It is interesting that Michiel does not seem to support the use of dried herbarium specimens, as not long before it was Luca Ghini who had had the innovative idea of pressing plants and sticking them into books, thus inventing the herbarium or *Hortus Siccus*.

The need for observation from life had been at the basis of the foundation of the Padua botanical garden at its inception, and so maybe Michiel's complaint that the scientific community continued to do work based on dried specimens was a warning that things were swinging too far away from the live plants. In 1544, the same year as he was writing to

Aldrovandi, Michiel moved away from Venice for four years to take up a position which involved the systemization of the plants in the Padua botanical garden. He had been invited there in recognition of his expertise and was instructed to maintain and increase the garden's stock. He worked with Luigi Squalerno, (c 1502–1570) known as l'Anguillara, a botanist skilled in the use and care of simples, who had been there since 1546. As well as the plants, Michiel made improvements to the design of the garden, having a protective wall constructed and creating systematic beds.

Michiel returned to Venice to his own garden in 1548 to continue his work on *I Cinque Libri de Pianti*. We find the reference and the paintings of the auriculas in *Libro Rosso I*. The plants are referred to as the *Zanicula nel Fruili*, and once again the name *Auricula ursi da semplicisti* (the Bear's Ears of herbalists) is only one of several used by Michiel, the others being *Semperviva da Volagari*, *Herba recciera da herbari*, and *Artoctos da greci*. Three plants are depicted. The leaves and roots look similar to those of modern auriculas. The truss is born on a long cowslip-like stem, but the flowers, illustrated in yellow, white and carmine, bear small tufty petals of a somewhat tubular formation.

The paintings for these books are by Domenico Dalle Greche, and it is true that some are imprecise. Some plants were drawn from life, some from herbarium specimens, and others, like the *Garofali* or clove plant, were simply invented. Many though, like the *Hermodatilo* or autumn crocus and the *Pistolochia*, are both accurate, showing the plant at different stages, and graceful.

So, when we look at these three *Zanicula* images, are we really seeing ancestors of our present-day auricula plant? It has been argued that they lack important auricula characteristics, especially regarding the petals, and a comment later made by the Jesuit botanist Giovanni Battista Ferrari (1583–1655) in *Flora overo cultura di Fiori*, his influential book on floriculture published in 1638, implied that the Italian climate did not really suit them. 'Bears Ears are plants typical of the cold north,' he wrote, 'of interest for their variety and

Facing page: Catherine.

once put to live in an appropriate soil they take root easily. In spite of this, they do not live long, being plants used to the cold and they suffer from our warm climate and rot.'

While it is true that auriculas would not flourish in the more southerly parts of the country (Ferrari spent most of his life in Rome) in fact the locations at which Michiel says the plants were found are all high alpine habitats, just the sort of areas where the auricula would flourish: the Fruili mountains of north-east Italy, on Mount Suman, in the high Alps of Pania, in Gorizia (or Gorita, where Mattiolus was city physician in the 1550s) and on Mount Salvatino.

Clusius

By far the most important of the group of sixteenth century botanical writers to discuss the *Auricula ursi*, however, was Charles de l'Écluse, or Clusius (1526–1609). Born in Arras, the son of a nobleman, he told Matteo Caccini in a letter of 1606 that he had been interested in nature even as a boy. Later his first course of study at the university of Louvain was law, but within a short time he made his way to Wittenburg to study under the theological reformer Philip Melanchthon (1497–1560). For Clusius was a committed Protestant at a time when religion played an incredibly important role in intellectual life.

It is almost impossible for us to grasp what this meant to scholars at this time. Intense religious division and strife provided the uneasy background to so many of their activities, especially publication. Massacres of Protestants took place in France in the 1550s, and religious wars continued until the end of the century. In England Catholic monarchs persecuted Protestants, and Protestant monarchs harried Catholics. In 1550 in Italy the Catholic Inquisition made a charge of heresy against Ulisse Aldrovandi of which he was extremely lucky to clear himself. Tortures of the most unpleasant kind were used to exhort confessions if the accused stuck to heretical views. Following his imprisonment Aldrovandi wisely changed his discipline to the less controversial botany.

To be of the right faith at the right time was thus crucial to advancement. To be of the wrong

faith at the wrong time could lead to trouble of the deepest kind. As we shall see persecution or its threat caused some scholars to retire from public life and live quietly on their country estates until the climate changed, others fled their own countries only to return when a monarch or regime of a different persuasion came to power.

Sometimes, though it would seem they could not win. In the reign of Henry VIII the British botanist William Turner (1508–86) was banished from England and his books banned when he joined the Reformation. He was able to return on the accession of Edward VI, but during the first years of Mary's reign his works were once again banned and he lost his job and almost his life. Once again he fled to the continent and only returned when Elizabeth I became queen. This enforced movement did however, have some hugely beneficial results: relationships were formed (William Turner became a friend of the celebrated Swiss botanist Conrad Gesner and his circle), correspondences initiated and knowledge – and plants – were disseminated far more widely.

Plants were seen as an escape route from religious persecution, and their study a safer and less controversial discipline. It was Melanchthon who for such tactical reasons, advised Clusius to change his discipline from law to the less contentious medicine-and-botany. Clusius then spent some time in Switzerland before setting off for Montpelier in France in 1551.

Montpellier was the foremost centre of medical and botanical knowledge at the time. The great professor Guillaume Rondelet (1507–66) took a more practical approach to the subject than many other teachers. Some thought his ideas too practical – he caused a scandal by dissecting the body of his own baby son when he died. Less controversially he also took his students on outdoor plant-hunting expeditions in search of simples, quite a new approach at the time. In Montpellier, to some extent religious differences could be forgotten. Rondelet was a Protestant but a tolerant and peace-loving one who had many Catholic friends. He had even worked for a time as physician to an eminent cardinal and travelled to Italy where he came in contact with influential botanists such as Ghini, and Aldrovandi.

CLUSIUS' CATEGORIES

Auricula ursi I (the yellow coloured bear's ear)
This is described as having 'leaves ... as if strewn with flour or powder ... with a central lateral stem & ten, twenty, thirty, flowers (sometimes more, if cultivated in gardens, where excessively luxuriant) ... with a sweet honey odour ... pale yellow .... each centre with a characteristic white circular ring, style between stamens sometimes prominent sometimes absent ... seed like primrose ... root thick'. As to where it is found, he continues: 'It grows in Sneberg, Neuberg, Etscher and in the Styrian mountains in the shadow of Mount Gleysenfeld. I have found it in abundance and much more luxuriant on a rock below the town of Medling (two or more miles distant from Vienna) where it looks to the North and whence women root cutters fetch bundles of the flowers and sometimes the whole roots'.

Auricla Ursi II (the red flowered bear's ear)
This is described as having 'between naked stalks two inches long or a little more ..., eight or more flowers together in ... a congested umbrel, similar to the former but larger, colour shining red initially dark as if stained, afterwards elegant and bright, a pleasing red purple, within ring pale and white, odour as former but less.' As to where this is found he says, 'This I have looked for in vain all over the highest slopes of the Provinces but I first spotted it in the well-tended garden of CVD Aicholtz, the Viennese physician and Professor an old friend and most cherished host of mine; the Professor had previously been given it by a certain noble lady', but from whence it had come Clusius was unaware. He later discovered that it 'grew in abundance in Innsbruck and neighbouring Alps'. [Note: *remember this noble lady, as she plays an important role in this story*]

Auricula ursi III (the variable coloured bear's ear)
This 'is to be found the slopes of the Tyrol especially the Kitzpil. Leaves smaller than above ... flowers borne in similar umbrels, red, yet somewhat spotted ... roots fibrous. He then adds, 'CVD Joachim Camarerius, the leading physician of the renowned Republic of Nuremberg first showed it to me'. [This was Joachim Camerarius the Younger 1553–1598].

Auricula ursi IV (the flesh coloured bear's ear)
This is 'smaller than second ... leaves above smooth and bright, lower whitish and veined, a little pungent and bitter, flowers similar to above ... colour dilute red, the ring grey and downy ... Discovered in Sneberg surviving on the ridges and frequent in the Styrian mountains'.

Auricula ursi V (the narrow leaf bear's ear)
This he describes as 'with pressed down thickened root, not dissimilar to fourth many whitish hair like fibres. Five or six narrow leaves succulent and fat ... compact leaflets, four or five elegant flowers, colour dilute red. Grows in mountains of Carinthia, Upper Styria and especially in Mount Taurus and the slopes of Judenberg. Flowers towards end of July when snow on summit is melting. This variety is very rare'.

Auricula ursi VI (the small bear's ear)
This is also of 'colour dilute red or flesh coloured, not dissimilar to fourth ... odourless ... inner ring white woolly pubescent without prominent style. Observed in 1574 on summit and ridge of Sneberg. Any additional vicinity I see it in will be recorded afterwards'.

Auricula ursi VII (the small snow flower bear's ear)
'This variety is found, although very rarely, in Taurus and Judenberg, it is similar in every way but with leaves a little whiter because it has flowers just as white as snow. Flowers the whole of July and August after snow melt, sometimes under snow and penetrates the snow surface that the sun's rays release'.

After leaving Montpellier, Clusius worked for a while as tutor and then spent brief sojourns in Paris and London where he went plant hunting with Mattias de L'Obel, or Lobelius (1538–1616), the Flemish physician who came to England 'for religion' and became botanist to James I. Clusius also met Sir Philip Sidney and listened to Sir Francis Drake talking about the New World. A little later he travelled to Spain and Portugal.

Travel is in fact one of the key factors in the Botanical Renaissance. 'If reading gives so much utility to scholars, travel gives them ten times more', wrote Ulisse Aldrovandi in his *Discorso*. Sixteenth century botanists and herbalists set off undaunted, whether on plant-hunting rambles up the local mountains or years-long voyages across the world in search of exotics. 'In their collective reminiscences, travel seems to be a virtual pre-condition to becoming a new sort of naturalist', wrote Paula Findlen in her excellent 1994 book, *Possessing Nature*.

In 1573 Clusius was invited by Emperor Maximilian II to establish and direct the Imperial botanical garden in Vienna. Maximilian had an avid interest in curiosities and plants, and his large collection reflected the enormous importance of his court in Europe. It was the habit of the Imperial Court to lodge foreign courtiers in private houses, and throughout his stay Clusius lived with Professor Aicholz and his wife Anna and they became close friends. The Professor was a keen gardener and owned a garden in the city centre and two more outside the city walls.

All the while Clusius, who never enjoyed the best of health, was incredibly active. He had acquired eight languages and was in correspondence with like-minded people from England, Hungary, Austria, Greece, Italy, Poland, Spain, Portugal, The Netherlands, France, Germany and Norway. It is interesting to note how wide-ranging his 300-strong list of correspondents was from a social point of view. It included princes, aristocrats and wealthy collectors but, as the fascination with nature rippled down through society, also physicians, artists, apothecaries, perfumers, middle-class garden owners and a number of women – all linked by their obsession with plants.

This craze for plants can even be seen reflected in the fashion of the period; botanical and zoological designs decorated fabrics and furnishings, and a 'cabinet of curiosities' or *wunderkammer* was an essential attribute for anyone of standing. The enthusiasm shown for plants by Clusius' correspondents, however, went far beyond mere fashion. Even the very aristocratic Marie de Brimeau Princess de Chimay, who called Clusius '*le père de tous les beaux Jardins du pays*' (the father of all the beautiful gardens in the country) was serious in her quest for knowledge, as were the Count of Arenberg and Lord Zouche, whose Hackney garden was famous in England.

Clusius was the undoubted master, and amongst the friends there was some rivalry as to who received the best specimens from him. This network would not only write letters but also visit each other's gardens and exchange plants, for which there was a strict code of 'give and take'. Credit due for cultivation or research should not be usurped and should be freely given. It was not done to be grudging with plants, and selling them to each other was seen as a betrayal of the camaraderie of connoisseurs. 'To hell with all this selling,' wrote Clusius in 1594.

Stealing of course was abhorred, but such was the desire to own a special plant that some people indulged in complex subterfuges. A visitor so craved a valuable anemone belonging to a Monsieur Bachelier that he went into the garden when the seed was ripe bearing a woollen robe which he bade his servant brush casually over the heads of the anemone so that some of the downy seeds would stick to the fabric.

By this time plants were discussed amongst herbalists in Latin, but the names were often long and unwieldy and could be altered at will. The wild briar rose for example was called *Rosa sylvestris inodorus sue canina* by some and *Rosa sylvestris alba cum rubore, folio glabro* by others.

Clusius travelled and wrote extensively. It is in a book about the plants in the vicinity of Austria, *Rariorum aliquot stirpium per Pannoniam, Austriam & vicini*, published in 1592 that we find his first references to the auricula, where he names seven

Facing page: Blossom Dearie.

types of *Auricula ursi*. In his longer work, *Rariorum Plantarum Historia*, of 1601, he adds a further two and changes some categories around.

Regarding the naming of the potential auricula it is of interest that Clusius begins, '*Non dubium est quin ad Primularum classen referenda sit venusta haec planta adeo smiles sunt & forma & temperamento* [There is no doubt that this attractive plant is to be referred to the class of Primula, such is its mimicking of them in appearance and temperament] thus at the outset comparing it with the primrose or *Primula veris* and so linking it with the genus to which it will later be assigned. He continues, 'I have observed many varieties of it on the Alpine slopes and I shall describe them in their proper place, beginning with the most well known though it is the most sweet smelling of all.'

Clusius says that some of these plants are mentioned by Simlerus (Josias Simmler whose 1574 commentary on the Alps *De Alpibus commentarius* summed up contemporary knowledge of the region), and some were collected by the great Swiss botanist Conrad Gesner. He continues that the ancients were ignorant of the names of these plants, but that Mattioli calls them *Saniculae* and Gesner *Lunariis herbis* or *Lunariam Arthriticam*, while another term is *Paralyticum alpinam*. Common people and students of herbs call them bear's ears. In Switzerland they are *Flublumle*, the little flower that consumes rocks, or *Craftkraut* and *Schwindelkraut* from the form of the rock. Goat and ibex hunters use the herb as they do the Doronicum root, for giddiness 'so as not to fall over into the abyss'. The residents of Medling near where it grows plentifully call it *Wolfmechende Schussel blumen*. The second and third types are called *Gotteschusse blumen* by residents. The fourth type is called *Stainroslin* or rock rose by mountain shepherds and the fifth, *hols Speick* which is horse balm furnished with spikes, by the mountain residents of upper Styria.

In the later book, *Plantarum Historium* 1601, the first four categories remain the same but some of the other categories have been swapped around and new plants now appear as *Auricula ursi V* and VI.

In these important early accounts of the ancestor plants of the auricula it is apparent that there were many species of alpine primula. By classifying them, Clusius did something which was useful throughout the next century – indeed 'C' indicating his provenance will be appended to references by many later herbalists. He also provided a plethora of synonyms and common names by which they were known and could be identified.

Auricula ursi however, was to remain the chief name by which the plant was known for many years. Caspar Bauhin (1560–1624), a Swiss botanist, in his 1623 *Pinax Theatri Botanici* refers to *Sanicula Alpina vel Auricua ursi* (Sanicula alpine or Bear's Ear) and quotes Gesner, Mattiolus and Clusius as to its provenance. Bauhin's landmark work describes some 6000 plants and classifies them in an early form of binomial nomenclature which to some extent predated Linnaeus.

The name *Auricula ursi* or its translation is still sometimes heard today. A photograph of a *Primula auricula* labelled *Orecchia d'Orso* seen in the Torino botanical garden was sent to me by a correspondent in 2009.

THE INFLUENCE OF LINNAEUS

The seventeenth century was a time of intense investigation. Plant hunters scoured their own countries for plants to document. Travel to far-flung countries resulted in the discovery of amazing plants previously unknown and unnamed. By the next century the need for structure and order became imperative to make sense of the proliferating plant families.

In Carl von Linné, or Linnaeus (1707–78) this need was answered. Linnaeus is recognized as the father of modern plant taxonomy, and his binomial system is still in use today although not based on his original principles of plant sexuality. In general, botanical names published before 1753 have no standing in modern nomenclature unless they were adopted by Linnaeus.

Linnaeus was a genius with an analytical mind, a strong visual memory and a supremely methodical way of working. A professor at Uppsala University in Sweden, he was also a good teacher who not

Facing page: Valerie.

Beatrice.

only instilled into his students a love of book learning but also took them on practical expeditions called *herbationes*. I myself participated in a reconstruction of one of these walks in Uppsala at the time of the Linnaeus tercentenary, crossing the wide King's Meadow covered with fritillaries and following the Danmark path to Sävja, a small farm which belonged to Linnaeus, where after gathering specimens he and his students would pause for breakfast. These jaunts inspired many of his pupils to go on and take up lives of plant-hunting all over the globe. In some of his books he broke with the tradition of writing in Latin and used a simple, almost poetic, vernacular Swedish, and the books which dealt with his journeys throughout Sweden proved especially popular.

Extremely influential, not to say controversial, was the system he published classifying plants based on their sexuality, that is, according to their pistils and stamens. 'Love comes even to plants', he wrote, using some rather quaint, and to some ears, shocking, 'marriage metaphors' to describe plant reproduction. 'The flowers' leaves … serve as bridal beds which the Creator has so gloriously arranged, adorned with such noble bed curtains, and perfumed with so many soft scents that the bridegroom with his bride might there celebrate their nuptials with so much the greater solemnity.'

Critics accused Linnaeus of botanical pornography, saying that his books were unfit for the eyes of women. They did, however, undoubtedly encourage an interest in botany in many who had never before given it a thought – especially women.

'Botanizing' in fact, became a passion throughout Europe from Royalty downwards. Linnaeus, whose self-confidence was rock solid, was never fazed by adverse comments. He believed that he had been put on this earth with the purpose of making sense of the creation. 'God creates but Linnaeus orders', was one of his modest claims.

The Binomial System

The sexual classification of plants was eventually superseded, but Linnaeus' lasting legacy is the binomial system which has ever since permitted botanists and gardeners to communicate world wide. In fact he was not the first to use a binomial system, but he was the most consistent – and the most published. In his system he used one Latin word, 'the true phrase-name' or *genus* for the family group of the plant, to which he added the description of the individual family member which became known as the specific epithet or *species*.

The concept of the genus was not new. It had been used extensively by the French botanist Joseph Pitton de Tournefort (1656–1708). Linnaeus however, did not make extensive use of Tournefort's nomenclature. He did not like a two-word genus, and amongst the changes he made was a shortening of Tournefort's *Primula veris* to *Primula*, which had consequences we shall examine later. Linnaeus preferred his generic names to be 'as short, euphonious, distinctive and memorable', as possible. To this end he made use of some classical terms, but in the main he delighted in inventing genetic names himself, sometimes honouring colleagues and friends, for example naming the *Rudbekia* after his old mentor Olof Rudbeck the Younger, and the *Cliffordia* after George Clifford for whom he had worked in Holland. He even had fun in using the names of people he did not like for ugly or unpleasant plants. Johann Siegesbeck, who denounced Linnaeus' plant sexuality system as 'lewd and loathsome harlotry' is remembered in an insignificant weed *Siegesbeckia orientalis*.

Facing page: Cinnamon.

Originally, even Linnaeus himself did not restrict the specific epithet to one or two words; in some cases it could run to a dozen. Soon however, he realized that there was little use for such long names outside learned books and so devised a single catch phrase, a sort of shorthand form, which he first called *nomen triviali*. It is this 'trivial name' which originated as notes scribbled in the margins which eventually became the second leg of what was to be binomial nomenclature. This of course simplified matters considerably – in *Species Plantarum* we see the wild rose has become the much more manageable *rosa canina*.

Of significance to our story is the fact that Linnaeus had his own ideas as to genera and often discarded names assigned by previous botanists. This did not always go down well. His contemporary, the German Johann Jacob Dillenius (1687–1747), Sherardian Professor of Botany in Oxford, wrote to him in 1737, 'We all know that botanical nomenclature is an Augean stable which … even Gesner was unable to cleanse. It is a task requiring much reading and wide and deep learning, and should not be undertaken precipitously or carelessly; you rush in and overturn everything.'

Rushing in, Linnaeus discarded the name *Auricula ursi* and the other associated names of our plant and taking from Tournefort's *Primula veris* the single word *Primula* as the genetic name, probably because our plant also blooms early in the spring and, as Clusius had noted, has similarities 'in appearance and temperament', he reassigned it to the genus Primula. The *Auricula ursi* or Bear's Ears thus found itself one of several divisions into which Linnaeus split the genus Primula.

Was this a good move? Considering that today the genus Primula is one of the most variable in the world, and now about 500 species of *Primula* have been recorded, and the section *Auricula* is one of 37 sections of the genus and one of three sections of the subgenus Auriculastrum, we might conclude that searching for the true ancestors of today's cultivars within such a huge family is a daunting task. We might even come to the conclusion that Linnaeus' 'almost unparalleled discontinuity in botanical nomenclature … could be unfortunate.' That however, was the situation in which the auricula found itself post-Linnaeus.

VON WULFEN'S ASSUMPTION

The next development in the story came in the 1770s when specimens of an Alpine primula, probably Clusius' *Auricula ursi II*, were found by the Jesuit botanist Franz Xaver von Wulfen (1728–1805), who explored the Eastern Alps and made a study of the flora. Rather than finding the plants growing wild on the surrounding mountains however, he came across them in the gardens of the villagers of Windish-Matrei in East Tyrol.

Von Wulfen sent specimens of these primulas to his friend the Dutch botanist Nikolaus Joseph von Jacquin (1727–1817). Born in Leiden, von Jacquin was a family friend of the Mozarts and spent much time in Vienna where he became Director, first of Schönbrunn botanical garden and later of the botanical garden of Vienna. He was responsible for several books including *Flora Austriacae*. Believing that von Wulfen had found a true species, von Jacquin named it *Primula pubescens*. Searches were subsequently made in the Iselthal mountain area, but no more specimens were found, although some were observed growing in the gardens in the valleys of the Pasterthal and the Innthal in Northern Tirol.

KERNER'S DISCOVERY

It was not until 1867, by which date many other primula hybrids had been named, that the most significant breakthrough occurred, when Anton Kerner von Marilaun (1831–98), Professor of Natural History and Director of the botanical gardens of the University of Innsbruck, found two primulas that revealed to him a new story. Kerner was a keen alpinist and plant hunter who had set up an experimental station in the Blaser above Trins in the Gschnitz Mountains, where he spent his summer holidays. One day on one of his expeditions in this area he found two primulas, *Primula auricula* and *P. hirsuta* (now *P. rubra*), growing adjacent to each other, species which basically require quite different edaphic (environmental soil) conditions.

Facing page: Maureen Millward.

The yellow *Primula auricula* occurs above the tree level on limestone rocks. There is some variation, but in general the plant is somewhat like a cowslip with a truss of slightly trumpet-shaped flowers growing in a cluster on the top of the footstalk and importantly, often bearing a dusting of paste or farina on the leaves which are thicker and more succulent than those of many other primula species. A thin layer of the pigment flavin near the surface of the petals accounts for the yellow colour.

The smaller, reddish *P. hirsuta* normally prefers the more acid silicate or granite and is usually found embedded in north-facing rocks. It has sticky green leaves bearing tiny hairs that have a characteristic smell but bear no farina. Its flowers are round and flat rather than trumpet shaped and range from pale pink to a deep maroon bordering on black. The colour in this species is derived from the pigment hirsutin which produces the wide range of colour as it changes according to the acidity of the sap which is found in the middle of petals.

Recognizing that this yellow *Primula auricula* is undoubtedly the plant referred to by Clusius as *Auricula ursi I*, Kerner also remembered that Clusius had written of one of his auriculas, *Auricula ursi II*, that it had been obtained from a 'noble lady' and that he Clusius had searched in vain for it all over the Austrian Archduchy and later discovered that it had come from the mountains somewhere near Innsbruck.

Kerner then worked out that this 'noble lady' could have been a certain Countess Trautmannsdorf, one of Clusius' correspondents who had been in the habit of spending vacations at her summer property Schloss Trautson, a castle not far from Matrei where Wulfen had found the first plants.

It was by observing that in this region both acid and limestone rocks are found bordering each other that Kerner eventually deduced that although an uncommon occurrence, these two had successfully hybridized to form *Primula x pubescens* 'Jacq', the hybrid von Wulfen had found and which had been named in the previous century for von Jacquin on the assumption that it was a new species.

Kerner came to the conclusion that this plant *Primula x pubescens*, a fertile hybrid, should really be regarded as the correct name for the ancestor of all our auriculas. Thus he confirmed the pedigree of the only alpine plant to have become a cherished and valuable florists' flower.

It must be said that this news was not universally accepted, and when it was published in a paper in 1875 in England there were a number of objections from auricula enthusiasts. Shirley Hibberd (1825–90) author of *Garden Favourites*, believed that Alpine and Show auriculas had separate origins, and a Mr J.G. Baker claimed that rather than *P. x pubescens* 'Jacq' being the ancestor of all garden auriculas, it was only involved in the Alpine auricula, while the garden auricula owed its parentage to a variety of other primula species.

RECENT DEVELOPMENTS

As a rider to this, in the 1980s Dr Frank Taylor, a noted horticulturalist whose work in micro-propagation of auriculas at Wye College is well documented, had the idea of attempting, with the benefit of modern biotechnological techniques, first to recreate the hybrid *P. pubescens* from plants of *P. auricula* and *P. hirsuta* obtained from Switzerland, and then, when this plan was shelved, to reverse the situation and put the clock back 350 years by mutating some modern cultivars 'back to *P. pubescens*-like ancestors'. This research was halted in order to undertake more urgent micro-propagation, so unfortunately there were no conclusive results.

As we have seen, Clusius himself classified these *Auricula ursi*, thinking they were wild species plants. We now know that a great many more species and subspecies of *Primula auricula* do occur, some endemic to the mountainous areas from which variations of the potential florists' auriculas could have developed. With the benefit of hindsight we also know that natural primula hybrids pose problems for the taxonomist. According to Josef Halda, 'Some remain stable for many years while others continue to develop and furthermore they change chromosome numbers surprisingly quickly thus ruling this out as method of classification.'

Facing page: (clockwise) Primula hirsuta, P. auricula, P. pubescens.

Even now new species are being discovered which might possibly have had an input into the genetic make-up of our auriculas. In 1983, for example, the unexpected discovery took place of a new species *Primula recubariensis* endemic to the Piccole Dolomititi. Similar to *P. hirsuta*, to which it was first attributed, but with violet coloured flowers and found growing amongst non-siliceous rocks, it was subsequently recognized as a completely new species. A similar discovery was the very mealy *P. albenesis*, found high in rocky crevices in the Italian Alps in 1993. Then, even as recently as 1998, another was described, *P. grignensis* from the Grigna Merdiodionale, a tiny plant with pale pink flowers with white centres which is even said to hybridize with *P. auricula* in the wild.

Thus although hybridization with other species and subspecies may have played a part, it does seem likely that the varied genetic make-up of *P. hirsuta* and *P. auricula* went at least some of the way to accounting for the magnificent range of colour and form which subsequent hybridists have tapped into in order to create (and re-create in the case of doubles and stripes) the exquisite array of modern auriculas we enjoy today.

So, as it is now too long ago for us to be one hundred percent certain of the names of all possible ancestors of our plant, I leave the great C. Oscar Moreton the last word: 'It is perhaps a good thing that the veil of obscurity which is drawn over the past is not completely torn aside, for a certain sense of mystery is an essential part of beauty.'

Chaffinch.

CHAPTER 3

Out of the Wild and into the Garden

At some stage towards the end of the sixteenth century the auricula began its move out of the wild and into the garden. Until this time wild plants were gathered by country people to use for minor ills, herbs were cultivated in the monasteries from where the monks dispensed medical care to the sick, and food crops were grown to feed the population. Beyond this, serious interest in plants was not commonplace.

Of course flower gardens did exist in earlier centuries, and as M.M. Mahood says in her 2008 book, *The Poet as Botanist*, we can see massed flowers 'blossoming in the margins of Books of Hours and springing up with other *milles fleurs* between the hooves of tapestried unicorns, or at the feet of the Virgin in her *hortus conculus*'. Boccaccio described a flowery mead in the *Decameron* as 'a meadow, the grass of the deepest green starred with a thousand various flowers', an appealing image which is still something of a gardener's ideal today.

In Britain the number of gardens began to increase dramatically after the Wars of the Roses until the great Tudor gardens of Henry VIII at Nonesuch and Hampton Court were seen as potent expressions of the affluence and prosperity of the nation. Magnificent, well-structured gardens were also found in palace gardens throughout Europe, as well as in India, Persia and Turkey.

All these grand gardens were part of the furnishings of aristocratic life, however, and did not arise from the fascination verging on obsession with plants which was about to sweep through society from top to bottom as plants began to acquire decorative and ornamental values in their own right.

IN ITALY

Italy was one of the first European countries to establish great gardens. The Renaissance villas of the fifteenth century were laid out in magnificent style often inspired by the Roman ideal of life in the country, and this, coupled with a climate favourable to flower cultivation, meant that the Italian garden aesthetic was advanced. The paintings of Botticelli, such as *Primareva,* which depicts Chloris becoming Flora, Goddess of Flowers, for example, show exquisite and realistic depictions of flowers.

Thus, in tracing the journey of flowers, including the auricula, from the wild into the garden, it is perhaps not surprising that Italy should be in the vanguard. The fact that structure and design were fundamental to the Italian garden has to some extent obscured the fact that flowers were highly valued. The 1638 volume *Flora overo cultural di Fiori* by Giovanni Battista Ferrari even contains the first references to arranging flowers for interior decoration.

We have seen that Pietro Antonio Michiel published the first illustrations of auriculas in *I Cinque Libri di Piante*, but this book is also of interest because although it does mention the virtues of the plants, it was clearly not a work intended purely for physicians and apothecaries as such books had been in the past. Nor was it a treatise devoted either to cultivation or classification. In this work Michiel is seeing the plants as decorative, useful adjuncts to the garden. It is effectively a florilegium.

Michiel was interested in garden architecture, and his San Trovaso garden was considered one of the most exquisite of the Venetian Renaissance gardens then in the city. According to Dottoressa Susy Marcon, to whom I am indebted for much of this information on Michiel, 'the garden at San Trovaso was very well known for the quantity and singularity of the plants'. Conrad Gesner mentions it approvingly in his *De Hortis Germaniae* of 1561, and the great Mattiolus judged the garden, 'noteworthy not only for the exotic plants you find there but also for the aqueducts and rare grottos made with incredible artistic skill.'

In Michiel's *Libro Azzuro* some of Domenico's illustrations go way beyond the scope of the herbal. They are colour paintings that show trees in a garden embellished with architectural features. One shows a fir tree growing in a square maze surrounded by a trellis with an archway or pergola on which roses climb and birds flutter. There is no perspective in this painting, but it has a lot of charm. As well as the fir tree, which is seen in outline, a large sprig of foliage is depicted more realistically beside it, as if for identification. In another illustration, a *Philirea* is seen growing in a square raised bed in a garden surrounded by a low decorative wall pierced with niches and a doorway. Once again a sprig of foliage appears alongside the image. The third illustration is more elaborate and less realistic, as the tree, an *Acacia*, is placed, rather than planted, on an area of red and white chequered paving around which runs a high wall with arcades and decorated pillars. Lastly there is a beautiful example of topiary: a bird with wings outstretched, clipped from a myrtle planted in an urn.

We cannot be sure if these depict Michiel's own garden, as it no longer exists, but Lucia Tongiorgi Tomasi, in her 1997 book, *An Oak Spring Flora* comments that Michiel 'commissioned Domenico dalle Greche to paint hundreds of the plants growing in *his garden*', and certainly paved areas such as those shown were a feature of Venetian gardens of the time. Michiel's garden was one in which not only fellow botanists but also literary and artistic figures of the age gathered to walk and talk. It was a pleasure garden, and what is indicated in these books is a taste for using plants to create beautiful gardens. Thus it is does not seem too great a leap of imagination to picture the fledgling auriculas, brought down from the mountains

for acclimatization, growing happily in a corner of this important Venetian garden.

CLUSIUS AND HIS CIRCLE

It was Clusius, however, who according to Anna Pavord, 'Single-handed, transformed the appearance of gardens in Northern Europe, introducing many of the most precious delights of Renaissance flower beds'. He certainly played a key role in the dissemination of the auricula. From his books we learn that he tried acclimatizing these alpine primulas with varying results, and that he also passed them on to the friends in his network.

He described *Auricula ursi I*, the yellow mealed plant from Medling near Vienna, saying that the local herb women gathered flowers and roots to sell in the Viennese market each year. Many of these were apparently bought by Viennese ladies to plant in their gardens. He also speaks of a red flowered plant with smooth green leaves, his *Auricula ursi II* which he first spotted in the 'most well tended garden' of Dr Aicholtz with whom he lodged in Vienna and who he described as 'old friend and most cherished host'. (This is the plant Aichloz had received from the noble lady.)

The third type, *Auricula ursi III*, a smaller plant with red, somewhat spotted flowers which came from the Tyrol, particularly the Kitzspil, was the one Clusius had seen in the Nuremberg garden where his old friend C.V.D. Joachim Camerarius (1534–98) cultivated many rare plants. They had met as students at Wittenberg, and corresponded for over thirty years. Camerarius had even given Clusius some little seedlings on his way back from Belgium in 1579, but these had perished on the journey. In 1581 when on his way back from a trip to England Clusius once again visited Camerarius' garden and was given some more plantlets, but these too wasted away. The fifth, very rare, variety was brought down from the far-off mountains and survived for a few years in the Aicholtz's garden, but in the end it rejected all attempts at acclimatization

Facing page: Argus.

and never produced a flower. The sixth, the snow variety from the Taurus, on the other hand, according to Clusius would, if transplanted into a garden, flower in April and sometimes again in autumn if the weather was mild.

Clusius sums up by saying that although some had either faded away or did not flower, he was the first person to bring these very rare plants to Belgium where he distributed them to Johann de Brancion, 'a very dear friend … like a brother' and, after his death, to a relation of his, Johann van der Dilft and several other friends. He also comments that a Dr Alphonsius Pancius, physician of Ferrara, had already sent the plant with the yellow flower (presumably *Auricula ursi I*) to Belgium.

In his *Rariorum Plantarum* written nine years later, there are further mentions of these plants in a garden context. They include an *Auricula ursi* flowering in 1591 in 'the cultivated garden of the illustrious Prince Wilhelm IV of Hesse-Kassel'. Prince Wilhelm was a polymath who owned a large garden on the river Fulda where Clusius had worked occasionally as court gardener between 1588 and 1592. Another auricula was mentioned in the 'well tended garden' of 'that most noble gentleman Stephen Sprengerus'. This is of particular interest because not only did Philipp Stephan Sprenger, who was court chemist at Heidelberg, have an important collection of flowers (the catalogue made in 1597 shows three *Auricula ursi*), but his garden was also 'a formally arranged garden with complex decorative elements' including a labyrinth.

In his correspondence we find even more references to auriculas in garden settings. On 14 April 1587 he writes to Camerarius that he will send him a wooden box containing 'some sprouting horse chestnuts, some red flowered *Primula veris* and some auriculas'. Between 1588 and 1592 he also corresponded with Anna Aicholz, advising his old landlady who, after the death of her husband, struggled to maintain his gardens. In December 1593 Willem Parduijn, an apothecary of Middleburg, wrote to him in Leiden about a large leaved auricula he had seen in a garden in his town which he thought might have come from Constantinople or Italy. Middleburg, on an island on the coast of Zeeland, was a port at which

many exotic plants were disembarked, and was a centre of floriculture and rich with gardens, several owned by Parduijn. Middleburg incidentally was where Lobelius had been a one-time town doctor. Another of Clusius' correspondents, also a friend of Lobelius, was Jacques Plateau of Tournai, a wealthy individual who owned a big garden. Two catalogues made of the plants in his garden in 1584 and 1586 show *Auricula ursi flo rubro et luteo*, red and yellow auriculas. In 1601 Joachim Levenier of Bordeaux wrote to Clusius of an *Auricula ursi* he had seen in a Paris botanical garden.

In all Clusius' exchanges the important word is *garden*. As more of these alpine primulas were cultivated it was found that *Auricula ursi II* threw more and more colours whereas the yellow mealy-leaved *Auricula ursi I* did not. Thus the native species fell out of favour as the cultivated forms of *Auricula ursi II* continued to proliferate and develop.

The timing was perfect. The auricula had come down from the mountain and into the garden at exactly the moment when a swelling wave of enthusiasm for floriculture was spreading rapidly across Europe bringing with it the desire for new and attractive plants. That the little *Auricula ursi*, or Bear's Ear, even in the comparatively simple form it exhibited at this period, was amongst the plants chosen to be treasured as a florist's flower is perhaps the principal reason why we have so many and varied cultivars today. For this we must thank Clusius.

He spent the last sixteen years of his life as professor of botany at the University of Leiden, which accordingly became the centre of his vast network from whence the auricula was disseminated swiftly throughout Holland, Belgium and Northern France.

FRANEAU'S ELEGIES

Effectively confirming the progress of the auricula is the contents of a charming little volume published in 1616 at Douai by a flower-loving gentleman lawyer, Jean Franeau, Le Sieur de Lestocquoy. Entitled *Le Jardin D'Hyver ou Cabinet des Fleurs* [*The Winter Garden or Cabinet of Flowers*] it consisted of twenty-four poems or elegies, together with some notes, describing the 'rarest and most outstanding flowers of the most floriferous borders'. Heading the elegized flowers were tulips, nearly always the collectors' favourites, but they also included *oreilles d'ours* [Bear's Ears].

Franeau begins by saying that beautiful gardens can be found in Brussels, Lille, Arras, Tournus, Tournay, Douai and Cambrai. He declares that gardening is a praiseworthy activity and gives as one of his objectives in writing this book: '*fermera la bouche à plusieurs qui meprisent les honestes plaisirs des jardins*' [to shut the mouths of those who despise the honest pleasures of gardens]. He makes the point that tulips for example were cultivated by '*les grans*', the Flemish elite, but that these nobles need not fear derogation, that is, losing their noble status by involving themselves in lowering activities because this sort of cultivation is, after all, a form of agriculture.

The title *The Winter Garden* is itself something of a poetic conceit. The flowers outside may be dead, hence the elegies, but they can still be enjoyed even when in 'the gardens & domestic parterres, amid the rigours of a rude cold winter, when ice, hail, frost and snow have made the earth bare and sterile and nature has withdrawn the flowers', because even then the author with his pen can provide glimpses of some of the most exquisite garden flowers for the reader to enjoy at his ease, as if from within the shelter of his 'Cabinet'. The use of the word 'cabinet' carries an echo of the cabinet of curiosities, the cupboard or room in which one's collection could be kept in perpetuity. A garden of rare flowers was often thought of as an outdoor museum of curiosities, and here Franeau claims the best of both virtual worlds – he brings the flowers of the garden cabinet into the literary cabinet of the book, to be preserved in perpetuity.

The elegies themselves follow the pattern familiar in seventeenth century poetry, in which the flower, a gift of Flora, is beyond the ability of a mere mortal to depict.

From this elegy and the notes which follow we can learn something of the auriculas of this period. That the colours are outstanding is apparent from the note in which Franeau compares them to silk. Silk was so highly esteemed in the seventeenth century as one of the most expensive

FRANEAU'S ELEGY TO THE BEAR'S EAR (IN TRANSLATION)

But who can do justice to Bear's Ears
when it comes to describing all their various shapes
their different features and their colours,
the whites, the yellows, the violets,
the russet tones, the reds and purples
which sweet Flora brings us in the springtime?
My pen is quite inadequate,
only a paint brush could capture them.
So go to these works of art, you silk workers from Milan
borrow their fine shades to delight the courtiers,
dip your silk stockings into tints like these
if ever your art is to imitate nature.
A stiff stem bears a cluster of flowers,
a perfect little bouquet made up of different colours.
Most beautiful of all, and unusual,
is the little moon in the centre of each flower.
I would describe it rather as a little sun
which shines in the middle with an extraordinary light.
It stands out best when the flower is *Brunette*
because within these little flowers,
which are like perfect nosegays,
if the petals are dark, those rays dazzle even more brightly.
And this is not all – our Flora decorates
these artistic bouquets in yet other ways,
some of them are edged and some have silvery trims.
So generous is Flora with her gifts and riches
offering all springtime's lovely bounty
with all the different types of foliage showing great variety.

and luxurious fabrics that in some countries only the elite had the right to wear it (Clusius himself compares flower petals to silver silk or silk shimmering with red and yellow threads). Franeau says that the best silk stockings come from Milan and invites the dyers to take note of the colours of the flowers of the bear's ears. Brunette, a rich brown, was obviously an esteemed colour which was found in the Bear's Ear called *Auricula Ursi de Poutrain*, Poutrain presumably being the raiser. He also draws attention to a more developed truss and the 'little moon' or eye.

In the conclusion to the book Franeau names places where any *curieux* (curious man) could see good bear's ears: chez M. le Docteur Morel at Douai and Monsieur Maitre Jean l'Eveque, '*homme fort curieux*' (very curious man) at Douai, thus providing evidence that even at this relatively early date florists were active in this area.

The term *curieux* was sometimes, as here, used almost synonymously with *fleuriste* which, as with the English term 'florist', referred to keen practitioners of floriculture of a selected group of flowers. Generally however, *un curieux* was a man of lively and cultured spirit whose interests could embrace antiquities, shells, minerals, and other curiosities of the natural world. A curious man loved to investigate all that was new and the strange. *Un curieux* was defined by the dictionary of the Academie Française of 1694 as someone '*qui a beaucoup d'envie et soin d'apprendre, de voir et de posséder des choses nouvelles, rares, excellentes, etc*' [who very much desires and cares to learn, see and possess new, rare and excellent things].

The curious enjoyed displaying the wonders of their cabinets of curiosities or *wunderkammer* to each other just as the florists loved showing off their plants. One of the differences however, is that the true florist, as well as displaying their plants, sought actively to 'improve' them and bring them to the highest degree of perfection. It is the idea of improving (and later hybridizing) which differentiated the true florist from the mere collector who simply purchased plants.

Another point of interest in *Le Jardin d'Hyver* is that on the frontispiece of this book, below the name of the publisher '*A Dovay de L'Imprimerie de Pierre Borremans à S. Pierre & S. Paul aet 1616*' are the names of two saints, Ste Dorothée and S. Théophile. It was quite usual to append names from the saints or the classics to books as a badge of status, and as this is obviously a Catholic initiative, saints are featured. Saint Théophile is

AURICULAS IN ANTONIUS GAYMANS' *HERBARIUM*	
Auricula ursi lutea h.l	Yellow Bear's Ear (*Hortus Leydensis*)
A. u. f. obsolete purpureo	Blush purple Bear's Ear
A. u. flore saturate purpureo	Deep purple Bear's Ear
A. u. flore m. purpureo rubente	Reddish purple Bear's Ear
A. u. flore aureo-purpuracente	Golden purplish Bear's Ear
A. u. flore minore candio	Small white Bear's Ear

probably mentioned because according to certain calendars his feast day is 5 March, and this book was published on 4 March. Sainte Dorothée owes her place here to the fact that she is the patron saint of gardeners and florists. It is interesting however, to note that this book predates, by over forty years, the formation of the official *Confrèrie de Sainte Dorothée* at which florists met.

Significantly for us, *Le Jardin d'Hyver* contains two engraved illustrations of auriculas by S. Serrurier, a full page showing twelve different sorts and another by the same illustrator showing a single flower. As line drawn engravings they lack the colour which enchants Franeau, but they show easily recognizable types of what we would call Border Auriculas.

GAYMANS' *HERBARIUM*

The visual appearance of auriculas of the period can be confirmed by looking at some which grew and were dried over four hundred years ago. These are to be found in the 1671 *Herbarium* of Antonius Gaymans (1630–80), a local pharmacist, at the

Facing page: Sword.

Rosalie Edwards.

Rikjherbarium in Leiden. Gaymans included two pages containing sixteen different types of auriculas. The colours have faded, and although one had a truss of seventeen pips it is not possible to see if paste was present. Categorized by colour, it is of note that the varieties of purples are quite sharply differentiated, indicating the intense interest in colour at the time.

BOTANICAL ILLUSTRATION

No herbarium specimen, however, can really rival the clarity of an accurate botanical illustration.

The coarse and frequently-used woodcuts of early herbals resulted in crude outlines and poor detail. Sometimes whole elements were omitted or became detached. Gerard, for example, writing about the blush coloured Bear's Ear in 1597, deplores the fact that the image shows no roots at all: 'the roote is tough and threddie, as are all the rest although the graver has omitted them in the cutting of the figure'.

Overall, the advantage of a more accurate representation made plant identification much easier. Copper engravings, even uncoloured (and a number were sold thus with the idea that the buyer could colour them in himself) were a vast improvement on woodblocks, as the technique resulted in more accurate detail achieved by hatching and stippling for shadow and the use of white space to simulate shine on leaves.

Woodcuts remained the main medium for book illustrations until the late sixteenth century. As Agnes Arber pointed out in her 1938 book *Herbals*, there was one advantage to the woodcuts which the newer copper engravings lacked: 'In wood cutting the lines are raised, and the method of printing is thus exactly the same as for type, while in metal engraving the lines are incised, so that the process is reversed ... .in a book of woodcuts there is no difficulty in keeping a just balance between text and illustration, which are printed together; on the other hand in a book with metal engravings which have to be printed separately ... the pictures are liable to lose their relation to the text'. She went on to compare woodcuts with photography, both of which she said, 'can be kept under firmer control'. This difficulty with process did account for a number of books in which the text was reduced to a minimum, as for example Emanuel Sweert's *Florilegium,* which we shall examine shortly.

Perhaps the greatest improvement occurred when the artists began to go directly to nature and draw or paint live plants. We see early evidence of this in Albrect Dürer who, working in the early sixteenth century, produced some outstanding plant portraits. His *The Great Turf* of 1503 depicts a piece of turf with grasses, speedwell and dandelions as seen from a worm's eye view, all of which are easily identifiable. His *Tuft of Cowslips* of 1526 is an equally faithful depiction.

We see it too in Hans Weiditz's illustrations for Otto Brunfels' 1530 *Herbarum vivae eicone* [*Living Portraits of Plants*]. The title itself indicates something of a new attitude, with some of the flowers depicted realistically with insect damage or withered leaves, a style which was to be adopted almost as a cult by some subsequent artists.

The images in Conrad Gesner's unpublished *Historia Plantarum,* some by himself and some by artists he employed, are also well observed, containing a wealth of extra information: seed heads, fruits, roots and written notes. Gesner had been preparing these illustrations over the last ten years of his life when, in 1565 he, like Mattiolus and

Facing page: Fanny Meerbeck.

Michiel, succumbed to the pitiless plague which raged through Europe.

Amongst the images in *Historia Plantarum* we find a plate depicting the *Auricula ursi* which shows a plant with a truss of five pips with smallish rather ill-shaped yellow petals and a white central eye. It has a large fleshy carrot with a sizeable offset attached to it and very recognizable and authentic-looking roots and leaves. Smaller drawings show the seed head and seed capsule. When we see the image there is no doubt we are looking at a simple Border type auricula. It is more convincing than Michiel's image of around the same date, and in fact it does more than just identify the plant: the extra details provide clues to its life history.

DECORATIVE PAINTINGS OF FLOWERS

In the seventeenth century botanical illustration in general was entering a new phase. We begin to see flowers depicted for their own sake rather than for information, as in herbals, or for iconic reasons, as in religious art. Images of flowers had long been associated with the Virgin Mary, and these especially appealed to Catholic sensibilities, but with the conflicts still raging between Reformation and Counter-reformation, in the seventeenth century wealthy Protestant merchants began to commission still life paintings of flowers to decorate their homes. Ambrosius Bosschaert the Elder (1573–1645), who painted flower pieces influenced by botanical studies, moved from Antwerp to avoid Catholic persecution. As Jack Goody puts it in his book of 1993, *The Culture of Flowers*, 'The Catholic couronne had given way to the Protestant bouquet'. Many of these contained auriculas. The French artist Jacques Linard painted easily identified auriculas of many colours in the 1640s.

In the seventeenth century there emerged two further illustrated media, the printed nursery catalogue and the florilegium. Although different in intent, these in fact fed into each other.

THE NURSERY CATALOGUE

As commercial nurseries developed, the trade catalogue became a powerful marketing tool. It was realized that, then as now, good pictures of plants could attract buyers from afar. At this period it is surprising how plants, aided by clever inventions, survived very lengthy journeys. Crispjin van de Passe the Younger (1589–1670) in his *Hortus Floridus* of 1614 illustrates a tubular container made from metal, the *Tubus ferreus ad Plantas transferedas*, in which tulips could be transported securely. G.B. Ferrari includes a similar picture of this and also an image of an ingenious travelling box, the *Capsula ambulatorio assere flores transferens*, which he had devised for despatching flowers. Both of these are illustrated in *Flora oveos cultura di Fiore* by Cornelius Bloemart.

Correspondence also reveals details of the journeys which plants undertook. Some were reasonably short, as in 1691 when Sir Thomas Hanmer sent a parcel from his home on the Welsh borders to John Evelyn in London with the note, 'I send you herewith some roots of several sorts, the bear's ears are very good … they will be a fortnight at least before they come to Deptford'. Others were considerably longer, as when the Duke of Palma sent jasmine, oranges and lemons from his gardens in Italy to the Netherlands by a mule train. These journeys, of course, were insignificant when compared with the voyages from the Tropics and the New World. In all cases, in commerce the race was on to furnish the curious with the plants they desired.

The two first editions, the 1612 and the 1614, of Emanuel Sweerts' *Florilegium* were in fact catalogues (they were said to have contributed to the phenomenon of tulipomania), although later editions resembled more closely true florilegia. Sweerts (1552–1612) was a Dutch herbalist and nurseryman who supplied Rudolph II in Vienna, and it was probably at the Emperor's behest that he prepared his first catalogue for the Frankfurt Fair. He was knowledgeable, he corresponded with many botanists and was probably quite wealthy. He was certainly a business man, and that he had an eye to the international market is shown by the multi-language index in which plants were named in Latin, German, Dutch and French.

At the beginning of the catalogue, which was in fact in the form of a large quarto book, he set out his sales pitch: 'Gentlemen if any amongst you desire to buy plants and flowers featured in this said book they will be found at the Fair in Frankfort at the shop of the author Emmanuel Sweerts, in front of the Römer, or Town Hall'. Then, not to lose any potential sales, he adds that afterwards they can be purchased from the establishment of his son-in-law 'Paulus de Ravenstein, printer of this book in Amsterdam' or from his own home on Bloemengracht.

He includes no text, placing sufficient reliance on the images to sell the plants. There are 550 copper engravings by different artists, including some directly copied from Johann Theodor de Bry's *Florilegium novum* (which in turn was copied from the French *Jardin du Roy* by Pierre Vallet; copyright did not apply to images in those days). One page contains drawings of six *Auricula ursi* together with some primroses. They are classed simply by colour: tawny, flesh coloured, white, yellow, red and purple, and are quite recognizable, if rather basic, specimens.

THE FLORILEGIUM

If Sweerts' first two catalogues represented the more mundane commercial end of botanical illustration, the florilegium proper represented the exclusive top end. The word 'florilegium', first used in this sense by the Flemish artist Adriaen Collaert in 1590, is a Latin term with exactly the same meaning as the word 'anthology', that is, a combination of the Greek words for 'flower' and 'collection' which carries the sense both of a composition, as of poems, and a collection, as of flowers.

The florilegia of the seventeenth and eighteenth centuries were usually impressive albums of paintings or engravings depicting flowers, often from the owner's garden. The wealthy and curious delighted in documenting their treasures, and for the owner of a significant plant collection it was a further sign of status to employ a good artist to portray them. The florilegium thus emerged as something the seriously curious man could use

in several ways. Looking at it he could, as indicated by Franeau in *Le Jardin d'Hyver*, mentally 'walk through his gardens' out of season; he could produce the volume to show to others of the same persuasion and thus show off his plants; and he could prove his wealth by the quality of the art which he had commissioned.

The fashion for florilegia gained momentum, and quite a number of them appeared around the same time. Not all were commissioned by private people. Some artists produced them by depicting flowers gathered from a number of sources.

Johann Theodor de Bry (1561–1623) was a Lutheran born in Liege, who later moved to Frankfurt, a safe haven for Protestants at this time. His *Florilegium Novum* using copper plates was first published in 1612 and consisted of images of flowers growing in Frankfurt gardens. He based his work on that of Pierre Vallet, who depicted plants cultivated in Henri IV's garden in Paris in *Le Jardin du Roy tres chrestien Henry IV Roy de France*, and the five auricula images are the same as in that work. This florilegium went though several editions, and an updated version *Florilegium Renovatum* was published in 1641 by his son-in-law Mattias Merian.

Hortus Floridus of Crispijn van de Passe the Younger (1589–1670), which appeared in English in 1615 as *A Garden of Flowers*, was one of the most popular florilegia ever created. It is divided into four books, one for each season. The Spring Book, in which the auriculas appear, begins with a delightful engraving of a formal walled garden with parterres, a gazebo and beds of tulips and crown imperials, and shows a woman picking flowers and an observer leaning on the balustrade. In the Winter Book the same garden is shown almost bare of plants. The individual flowers are charmingly depicted and decorated with little rabbits and birds. There are only two auriculas, a yellow and a violet, labelled in both Latin and Dutch.

The *Hortus Eystettensis*, prepared in 1613 for the super rich Johann Conrad, Prince-Bishop of Eichstatt by the apothecary Basilius Besler (1561–1629) is one of the earliest and finest of the florilegia. It is a very large book – Sir Thomas Browne referred to it as the 'massiest of the herbals' – which contains 367 plates depicting over a thousand plants. The Prince-Bishop's garden in Bavaria was a wonder of the world, considered the finest botanical garden outside Italy. His castle was situated on a rock with a river flowing below it, and his gardens, which he completely reoriented in order to display his flowers to their best advantage, consisted of eight separate gardens for different flowers, each tended by its own gardener. Many of his plants came from the Netherlands, and for the florilegium boxes of flowers were sent each week to the artists in Nuremberg.

This large-format book features three auriculas. Once again they are described simply by colour: purple, white and yellow. Beneath the images are the words *Bergsanicle* and *Bersanicle oder Flüssblumen*, to which a later hand has added: 'Primula auricula'. They are not great specimens, they bear trusses of five or six flowers with small petals, none of which show any trace of an eye. These auriculas are clearly only minor players in this vast work, which contains many exotic imported plants – but the fact that they are there at all shows that even at this early stage in their development they were numbered amongst the most desirable of flowers.

The Prince-Bishop died just before the florilegium was finished, but Besler had never intended the book to belong totally to his patron. Working with ten engravers Besler managed the production of a number of copies in two versions, black and white and coloured, which cost an enormous sum. 'I forebear to mention the engraver's wages', Besler commented. They did however become extremely collectable and formed a lasting memorial to the Prince-Bishop's garden, which was largely destroyed by the Swedes in the Thirty Years War which began in 1618.

A huge swathe of Europe was in fact destroyed during this war, but some parts of northern Germany suffered less and flowers continued to be painted for the eager collectors. One such was Duke Fredrick III of Schleswig-Holstein-Gottdorf, who in the 1650s commissioned a florilegium, known as the *Gottdorf Codex*, from the Hamburg artist Hans Simon Holzbecker. Painted on parchment it features a far greater number of auriculas than in the *Hortus Eystettensis* and their types are much more advanced. We see twenty-eight Castle

Gottdorf auriculas of various colours: whites, greys, a pretty lavender blue, pinks and a variety of stripes, all showing clear central eyes of white or yellow. The plants are painted in a very realistic fashion with leaves and in most cases, roots. Holzbecker also included auriculas in the *Husum* and the *Eberhard Anckelmann* florilegia. These however, may have been copied from the *Gottdorf Codex* and show fewer specimens, less accurately depicted.

THE FRENCH CONNECTION

In seventeenth century France auriculas quickly made their way to Paris, where flowers, especially the florists' flowers, were greatly appreciated. Jean Robin (1550–1629) for whom the *Robinia* was named, was gardener to Henri III, Henri IV and Louis XIII, and in 1601 he produced a catalogue of his collection, *Catalogus Stirpium tam indigenarum quam exoticarum quae Lutetiae coluntur a J. Robino botanico region*. Even at this early date we find auriculas growing in the royal gardens. They too appear in the catalogue, simply with colour names: a yellow, a white, a *subluteo* (a pale yellow) and a *vario* or mixed coloured.

In 1608 many of the rare and desirable flowers including auriculas grown in the king's garden were illustrated in the aforementioned *Le Jardin du Roy tres chrestien Henry IV Roy de France* by the artist Pierre Vallet. This time we see two different reds, a white and a purple (plus a borage-leafed plant, *Auricula ursi flore et folio boraginis myconi*, which is not really an auricula but it turns up regularly with them). Here, as in the *Le Jardin d'Hyver*, we once again encounter the conceit of 'preserving' the flowers within the book where they need not 'fear the cold breath of winter, nor the shock of winds, nor the harsh, drying and withering rays of the sun'.

Vallet (1575–1635) was in fact professional embroiderer to the king, and the flowers in this book were intended to double as needlework designs. The book is dedicated to Marie de Medici,

Facing page: Green Shank.

Femme Fatale.

wife of Henri IV, herself a keen needlewoman who surrounded herself with flowers to remind herself of her native Tuscany. '*Je vous offre les fleurs, si vous les regardez, vous y verrez les lys de France & de Florence que vous avez unis & bien contregardez*' [I offer you flowers; if you look at them you will see the lilies of France and Florence which you united and safeguard]. The volume also bears an advertisement addressed 'to those who wish to paint or illuminate or embroider or make tapestries from this book'.

That embroideries and garden design could successfully share the same patterns is endorsed by the fact that the term *tapisserie* [tapestry] could at this time be used as a synonym for garden. Marie de Brimeau, Princess de Chimay in correspondence with Clusius frequently referred to her own garden as a *tapisserie*, and she also commented to him that 'the riches of your tapestries surpass by far those of gold and silk as nature surpasses artifice'.

In 1656 Giuillaume Toulouze,'Maitre Brodeur de Mont-pelier' produced a *Livre des Fleurs, feuilles et oyzeaux* [book of flowers, leaves and birds] for professional embroiderers, and other books were used by jewellers and decorators. In France flower motifs as used by Le Brun at Vaux le Vicomte reflected the mania for florists' flowers. Flowery beams and flower-strewn ceilings known as *plafonds à la française* were to be seen in many a *hotel particulier*.

The craze for embroidery books was not restricted to France. In 1680 in Germany Maria Sybilla Merian (1647–1717), one of the greatest female painters in the history of botanical illustration, published her own floral pattern book *Neues Blumenbuch*. She was the daughter of the well-known engraver Matthias Merian, who was the son-in-law of Johann Theodor de Bry. Maria's book shows the influence of the French artist Nicolas Robert (1614–85), perhaps the finest botanical painter of the age. He had been chosen when still quite young to illustrate a sumptuous book, *La Guirlande de Julie*. In this volume, a present from Conte de Montausier to his fiancée Julie d'Angennes, leading poets, members of the famous salon organized by Julie's mother the Marquise de Rambouillet, composed madrigals comparing Julie's beauty advantageously to flowers. Overnight Robert found himself famous, and he was soon commissioned by Gaston d'Orléans, brother of King Louis XIII to paint a florilegium illustrating the flowers from the gardens of his chateau at Blois.

The Superintendent of the gardens at Blois was a Scotsman, Robert Morison (1620–83) a Royalist in exile, who had been severely wounded in battle in 1644. After the Restoration Morison returned to England, was appointed Royal Physician to Charles II and later went on to become the first Professor of Botany at Oxford. After his death Jacob Bobart the Younger (1640–1719) finished part of the great work Morison had planned to illustrate his taxonomic theories, but this was never published as a whole. Astonishingly, the original copper plates for the illustrations were discovered quite recently in use as counterweights to a lift in one of the university's libraries – a poignant example of the indignities significant items can suffer when fashions change. It is believed that during his ten-year exile in France, Morison was responsible for encouraging Robert in botanical painting. Watercolour painting on vellum was Robert's forte, and at the time of Gaston D'Orléans' death in 1660 he had

Facing page: C. W. Needham.

produced five large folio volumes, which were inherited by Gaston's nephew Louis XIV. Robert's depiction of the auricula is extremely graceful.

FLOWERS BESTOW STATUS

Enthusiasm for flowers continued to sweep through French society. It was, as in other parts of Europe, something which attracted those who were, or aspired to be, considered cultured. There are few things today which can compare with this social phenomenon. Maybe to own a collection of fine paintings holds something of the same cachet, and possibly 'galanthomania' (the current craze for snowdrops in England – where the price for one tiny bulb reached over two hundred pounds) reflects the financial heights to which connoisseurs will go, but neither quite encapsulates the social aspects of the seventeenth century floral obsession.

The thrill and excitement generated by flowers, especially among men, was specific to this period. That it came about has been linked with the advent of the tulip from Turkey, which is said to have brought with it the notion that from Suleiman the Magnificent downwards, the most important and cultured *men* in society venerated flowers. That it was mainly a masculine phenomenon is seen throughout Europe where, with a few exceptions, floriculture became a male preserve until the period post-Linnaeus when 'botanizing' was eagerly taken up by girls and women. That men embraced floriculture so readily in the seventeenth century is surprising in view of the fact that flowers had previously been associated with Flora and femininity. In France within the very male-dominated horticultural trade, women were relegated to such occupations as street flower-selling – and of course, weeding.

England, as we shall see, took a somewhat different view. Parkinson refers to a Mistress Thomasina Turnstall of Hornby Castle in Yorkshire as 'a great lover of these delights who hath often sent me up rootes to London'. Women also raised flowers, including auriculas, as we shall see, and even our Duchesses and some of our Queens enjoyed gardening. That being said, however, as soon as the idea of competition entered the story, even in England men took over: florists' feasts, in fact were reserved for the '*Sons* of Flora'.

In France the *curieux fleuriste* demonstrated his good taste, and to do so he involved other like-minded people with whom he enjoyed the fellowship and what Charles de la Chesnée Monstereul, author of *Le Floriste François*, a 1645 treatise on tulips, refers to as 'pleasant visits, gentle consultations and the firm support'. Monstereul makes a point of differentiating the French and Flemish florists, who instituted a town *confrérerie*, taking Saint Dorothy as patron, from the protestant Dutch who met 'to make a commerce of flowers' as if they were 'diamonds and pearls'. He also distinguishes the true florist from the *curieux ignorans* who 'possesses treasures without knowing their value'. The French florist however was someone who was seriously involved with his flowers, having some knowledge of their cultivation and appreciation of their place in the natural hierarchy.

The religious significance of flowers in this context was somewhat ambiguous. Sometimes flowers were interpreted as carrying the message of the *vanitas* – the passing beauty of earthly things and the need to prepare for life everlasting. Even Emanuel Sweerts' catalogue draws attention to the marvels of an all powerful God and suggests that in admiring and contemplating flowers man should remember the shortness and fragility of life. At other times, as the Puritans believed, the beauty of flowers was thought to distract from contemplation of God. The crash in the Dutch tulip markets in 1637 was seen by some as God's revenge on those who valued tulips more than Him or even put wealth before the *true* love of flowers.

In seventeenth and eighteenth century France, as quite a number of florists were priests – an occupation which afforded ample time to devote to plants – some writers from this milieu endeavoured to endow what was basically a worldly hobby with a deeper spiritual significance. In 1641 Père Leroy Allard wrote a book which he entitled *La Sainteté de vie tirée de la consideration des plantes* [The holiness of life drawn from the consideration

Facing page: Old Yellow Dusty Miller.

of plants] thus implying that plants were good for the soul. In the same vein Monstereul wrote: *'C'est offenser Dieu de mépriser les fleurs'* [It is an offence to God to despise flowers].

The florists nevertheless, saw no contradiction in their attempts to 'improve' these divine works and engineer exciting new variations in speckling, dappling, mottling and doubling of their flowers. The idea that nature could be improved was, in fact central to the thinking of the modern and curious man. Of course some of the methods employed to achieve the amazingly coloured, fantastically striped, copiously doubled or heavily scented flower do seem odd. It was believed, for example, that doubling could be achieved by planting at the full moon, that colour could be changed by adding tinted pigments when watering and that scent could be created by dousing with a complex solution of spices.

Another striking aspect was the fact that floriculture had a wide social appeal. From the days of Pierre Vallet the interest in flowers in France had been embraced by the highest in the land. It was Louis XIV, however, who took floriculture to the most dizzying heights. Paris became the cultural capital of flowers, and at Versailles vast quantities of select and rare flowers available were displayed in the most lavish fashion. The Trianon was known as the *Palais du Flore*, and extensive flower farms were developed to supply the quantities of blooms required. It was even thought that flowers would bring cultural rebirth after years of European wars and so bring honour and glory to France. France under Louis XIV was the undisputed leader of fashion and influenced what went on in all the other courts of Europe, but as Elizabeth Hyde pointed out in her 2005 book, *Cultivated Power*, the craze for flowers extended though all the affluent classes; it was not just question of what the king did filtering down through society, rather that the king caught the spirit of the age and harnessed it to increase his power.

The connoisseurs in France, as in Britain, fell into two categories. There were the *collectors*, mainly wealthy and educated men whose desire was to *acquire* delicious floral novelties, and the *growers* or true *fleuristes* whose aim was to *produce*

wonderful new plants. There were of course people who straddled both categories, nurserymen who avidly collected and gardening aristocrats who enjoyed growing plants. In France it was surprising that gardening became such a craze as this was a society where manual labour was not only considered lowly but could, as we have seen from Franeau, result in official *derogation*, which involved the loss of some of the aristocrat's privileges. When however, Gaston d'Orleans, the brother of the king, could be seen working in his garden at the Luxembourg Palace, it was clear that horticulture could be taken as a branch of agriculture, in which a landowner had always been permitted to indulge so as to maintain his estates, and was thus something that the rest of society could take up without fear of ridicule.

Louis XIV took advantage of this swelling enthusiasm, as Nicolas de Valnay, Controller of the Maison du Roi, tells us in his flower-gardening manual of 1688, *Connoissance et Cuture Parfaites des Belles Fleurs, Des Tulipes rares, Des Anemones extraordinaire, Des Oeillets fins et des belles Oreilles d'Ours panachées*: 'Before the reign of Louis XIV was the beauty of gardens known? ... he has brought forth flowers more beautiful than have ever been seen in order to serve as models to the clever architects of his trophies'.

Valnay puts auriculas in the top four of the fashionable flowers. Beautiful auriculas he describes as *panachées,* a term which means variegated or striped. When discussing where to obtain auriculas, the royal comptroller allows a hint of trade to creep in by directing his readers to specific gardeners, including himself, saying that he and a M. Descoteaux have the best collection of Bear's Ears in Paris.

Valnay also makes the claim that the Bear's Ear is French, although he adds, 'We are not the first to know their beauties. One must render justice to whom it is due, the Flemish are more attached to them than we; there are those who raised on the island in Flanders the first variegated ones; but after we purchased them, we have sown many are presently very rich in this flower'. It is not surprising that

Facing page: Harmony.

arguments as to who had bred the best auriculas were set to run and run.

This book brings the auricula right into the royal presence, as Valnay writes that in 1685, 'the illustrious and grand Curious, Monsieur le Chevalier de Saint Mory, sent the king a new striped auricula' and that ' His Majesty who admired (it), was surprised that there were such pretty flowers in the country which were unknown to him'.

With the death of the Sun King in 1715 the royal obsession with floriculture faded and the flower farms were abandoned. After this the French like the rest of Europe ordered their plants from the Dutch.

White Ensign.

CHAPTER 4

The Auricula Comes to England

THE HUGUENOT MYTH?

Tradition has it that auriculas were first brought to England from France by Protestant refugees fleeing religious persecution after the St Bartholomew's Day massacre in 1572. Amongst these refugees were Huguenot weavers and silk workers who settled in London, Lancashire and Yorkshire, and who were cited as the likely importers.

It has been argued by the late Ruth Duthie, a very reliable researcher, that this is unlikely, because at that date these plants were already expensive and thus beyond the means of humble folk. Further, no evidence has been found to corroborate this story.

The Huguenot provenance is found throughout the early literature about the auricula, so while it is not possible to prove, it is equally impossible to dismiss. The confusion may have arisen over the specific date, because as the European Wars of Religion continued over a long period, several waves of Huguenot refugees fled to England. The exodus which followed the St Bartholomew's Day Massacre was itself followed by a much larger one almost a century later, when the Edict of Nantes was revoked in France unleashing further persecution on the Protestants.

It is also worth noting that not all the Huguenot refugees were poor. Aristocrats and professional people were amongst them. As Bernard Cotteret said in his 1991 book, *Huguenots in England*, 'At the end of the seventeenth century several thousand Huguenot weavers, craftsmen, wig makers and artisans – not to forget their betters, pastors and gentihommes flocked to Britain'.

In those days, too, auriculas were mainly grown from seed, which was not expensive. A pinch of seed in a twist of paper would have been light and easy to transport, so although we shall never know for sure, it is not impossible that some of the early arrivals took some seeds into exile with them – something under the circumstances most of us who love auriculas would fully understand and try to emulate. The Huguenots were, after all, known to be people who brought great skills to English horticulture.

THE FIRST WRITTEN MENTION

We may not know exactly who introduced them but we know for sure that auriculas were growing in London gardens by 1596, as in that year John Gerard included them in the catalogue he published listing all the 1039 plants growing in his garden in Holborn in 1596–99. Dedicated to Sir Walter Raleigh, this catalogue was intended for circulation amongst his friends. It is a unique record of the contents of an Elizabethan garden at the time, and it contains the first written mention of auriculas growing in England, listing three types: *Auricula ursi flore purpureo, A.i flore luteo* and *A.u. flore vario* [purples, yellows and 'variables'].

As Stripes became so popular in the next century it is interesting to keep an eye on their development. Were these 'variables' mixed colours or really Stripes? Clusius in 1592 used the term '*Auricula ursi flore vario* for the plant with 'red, somewhat spotted' flowers. The Latin term 'varius' translates as 'party coloured, 'not the same in one place as another' or 'mottled' and so it *could* mean striped but it is important to know what it *did* mean historically. Here we cannot be sure.

Donhead.

What probably made these plants so popular, however, was the unexpected range of colours which these plants threw when grown randomly from seed. Elizabethans loved flowers and they loved colour. Wealthy people wore clothing lavishly embroidered with flowers. In the portrait by an unknown artist, *Elizabeth Vernon, At Her Toilet*, painted around 1600, we see the subject in a gown, embroidered with poppies, daffodils and other colourful flowers, which is open over her corset. In the famous Ditchley portrait of Queen Elisabeth I the 'flowers' were in fact made from jewels. Nor were men deprived of floriferous garments: the Hilliard miniature shows George Clifford wearing a particularly elaborate flower-encrusted jacket. Flowers also embellished Tudor furniture, tapestries and hangings. At Hardwick Hall, in anticipation of a visit by Elizabeth I, an allegorical frieze was made depicting Diana the virgin goddess amongst a medley of flowers, all chosen for their associations with purity.

Elizabethans also enjoyed elaborate conceits and floral similes – figures of words which were the verbal equivalent of the knot garden. Poets often compared flowers to the beauty of their mistresses as Henry Constable (1562–1613) does in his 'Of His Mistress Upon the occasion of her walking in a garden':

My lady's presence makes the roses red
Because to see her lips they blush for shame
The lily's leaves for envy pale became,
and her white hands in them this envy bred.

With such an appetite for flowers it was not surprising that England welcomed the 'strangers' or the 'out-landish', as exotic plants from abroad were called. One can imagine the vividly coloured little Bear's Ear appealing strongly to both men and women.

EARLY GARDENING MANUALS

Gardens were gradually becoming accessible to more people, and a number of 'how to do it' gardening books were published at this time. Thomas Tusser's 1557 *One Hundred* (expanded in 1573 to *Five Hundred*) *Good Points of Husbandry* was written entirely in easy-to-remember rhyme, as in: 'Good tilth brings seedes. Evil tilure, weedes'.

Two more charming early manuals are Thomas Hill's *The Gardener's Labyrinth* of 1577 and William Lawson's *The Countrie Housewife's Garden* of 1617. Lawson's is notable particularly as it was written by a practical gardener, and it is not aimed at the wealthy with a large staff of gardeners, but rather to garden owners and housewives who might actually get their hands dirty: 'If you be not able, nor wiling to hire a gardener, keep your profits to yourself, but then you must take all the pains.' He also offered useful advice: 'Physic holds it possible, that a clean body kept by these three Doctors, Doctor Diet, Doctor Quiet, and Doctor Merryman, may live neer a hundred years.' Lawson confirms the changing focus from the utilitarian to the decorative garden, ending with the often quoted remark: 'What was Paradise? but a Garden, an Orchard of Trees and Herbs, full of pleasure, and nothing there but delights.'

JOHN GERARD'S *HERBALL*

The first edition of John Gerard's *Herball or Generall Historie of Plantes*, perhaps the best known of British herbals, was published in 1597. John Gerard was not an academic, and in fact at the time no British university had faculties for the study of

Facing page: Walton Heath.

WHAT DOES GERARD SAY ABOUT AURICULAS?

In this 1597 edition, his chapter *Of Beares eares or Mountain Cowslips* begins: 'There be divers sorts of Mountain Cowslips or Beares eares, differing especially in the colour of their flowers, as shall be declared notwithstanding it may appear to the *curious* that there is great difference in the rootes also.' (Here we see that the term 'curious' was in use in England just as *curieux* was in France at the time.)

He lists eight plants and illustrates seven. The last two of these, *Auricula ursi minima*, the Stamell Beare's eare (stamell is 'a red inferior in brilliancy to scarlet') and a white version thereof, are tiny plants which we would not recognize as auriculas.

Of the first plant he says: 'This beautiful and brave plant, hath thicke, greene and fat leaves somewhat finely snipt about the edges, not unlike those of Cowslips but smoother, greener, and nothing rough or crumpled: among which riseth up a slender round stem a handful high bearing a tuft of floures at the top, of a fair yellow colour, not much unlike the flours of the Ox-lips, but more open and consisting of one only leafe like Cotiledon; the root is very threddy, and like unto the Oxe-lip.' This would clearly seem to be what we now call *Primula auricula* and what Clusius called *Aurucla ursi I*.

This is followed by a purple, the flowers of which have 'some yellowness in the middle' but are not as 'laid open' as the former.

Then come two reds, the first of which Gerard believes to be Clusius' *Auricula ursi II* and the second, which he calls Scarlet Beares Ear, Clusius' *Auricula ursi III*. The flowers of the first, the Red Beares Ear, are 'more shining within' while the outside is 'of the colour of a Mulberie', with a whitish eye in the middle. The flowers of the Scarlet 'are shining about the edges', with an 'overworne colour' towards the middle 'and a fork covered with hairiness' in the centre.

Next Gerard describes 'The blush coloured Beares eare' with smooth leaves of a whitish green colour, a whitish stalk with cowslip-like flowers of a whitish colour tending to purple 'which we term blush colour'. He describes all the roots as 'tough and threddie' (this is the specimen about which he complains that the engraver has omitted the roots).

His sixth example, the 'bright shining Beares-eare of Mattiolus description' he believes does not exist, considering it 'a figure foisted for ostentations sake.'

Gerard's are the earliest descriptions we find of auriculas growing in British gardens. From these descriptions we get impressions of bright and varied colours, of differences in the eyes, of different types of leaves and the presence of meal. He tells us that they grow naturally upon the 'Alpish and Helvetian mountains' and that now most of them grow in our London gardens. He offers some synonyms, and counts amongst their virtues those of healing and for giddiness, saying that those who hunt in the mountains for goats and bucks esteem them as they prevent 'the losse of their best joynts (I mean their neckes) if they take the roots before they ascent high places'.

Gerard died in 1612, his book having done extremely well.

plants. The only botanical gardens were those belonging to private individuals and Gerard, who was Master of the Company of Barber Surgeons in London, supervised two such, both belonging to Lord Burghley: one in the Strand in London and the other the great country gardens of Theobalds, near Waltham Cross, where Lord Burghley entertained Queen Elizabeth I. Gerard also had charge of the garden of the College of Physicians, as well as owning what he describes as the 'little plot of myne own especiall care and husbandry'. There, according to George Barker, the Queen's surgeon, he grew 'all manner of strange trees, herbes, rootes, plants, flours and other such rare things as

Facing page: Brookfield.

would make a man wonder how one of his degree, not having the purse of a number could ever accomplish the same.'

Although not a scholar, Gerard had a number of influential friends who, to some extent, kept him in touch with the European botanical network. These included Richard Garth, one of Clusius' correspondents; Jean Robin, the King of France's botanist who sent him seeds; Camerarius of Nuremberg and Lobelius, with whom he had a stormy relationship for reasons which we shall see.

If people have only heard of one British herbal it is invariably Gerard's, yet ironically this famous book was not exclusively his own work. A translation of *Pemptades* by the French physician Rembert Dodoen's (1517–58) had been undertaken for Norton, the Queen's publisher by a Dr Priest of the College of Surgeons, but he died before the work was finished, and Gerard, as garden curator, was asked to complete it. He claimed in his preface that Dr Priest's translation had perished with him, but this was quite untrue as he made use of most of it and simply changed the layout before claiming the whole book as 'the fruits of these mine own labours'.

In his *Herball*, Gerard was somewhat more inclined to fable and fantasy than to scientific truth, something which may have earned him readers but not the approbation of his more erudite contemporaries. (He includes, for example, the story of the barnacle tree, which was thought to bear eggs from which geese hatched.) Lobelius, who had settled permanently in England, found over a thousand errors, which Gerard refused to allow him to correct. He also found sections plagiarized from his own work *Stirpium adversaria nova*. To add to the confusion, some of the illustrations were attached to the wrong plants.

Nevertheless the end result, written in simple poetic language, gives us, through Gerard's fresh and beguiling descriptions, an insight into the real pleasure that the Elizabethans derived from flowers.

JOHN PARKINSON'S *PARADISUS*

In 1629 another great book was produced which gives the most comprehensive description of auriculas to date. This was *Paradisi in Sole, Paradisus Terrestris* by John Parkinson (1567–1650). Parkinson was an apothecary and a Catholic. The title translates as 'Park-in-Sun's Earthy Paradise', a pun on his own name, which puts him right in the centre of his own garden. For this book, subtitled 'A Garden of Pleasant Flowers', is above all one gardener's celebration of plants, for the benefit and pleasure of other gardeners.

At this time cities were expanding, and the vision of a landscape full of wildflowers which had sufficed for generations was now denied to many people. These were also uncomfortable times in which to live, especially in London. Plague had raged there in 1625, and in the same year as the *Paradisus* was published the animosity which had been simmering between Charles I and his Parliament came to a head, resulting in the King's dissolving Parliament and embarking on his years of Personal Rule. In such times the need for people to create their own versions of paradise becomes even more pressing, and more people began to appreciate plants for their form and beauty.

It is in describing these enthusiasts that we first come across the term 'florist' in England. In 1623 Sir Henry Wotton (1521–87) – poet, spy and ambassador in Venice for James I (he is credited with defining an ambassador as 'an honest man sent to lie abroad for his country') and flower-lover – was writing of 'having made the acquaintance with some excellent florists (as they are stiled)'. Sir Henry's brother employed the great horticulturalist John Tradescant the Elder (about whom we will see more later) at this time on his Kent estate and was later a benefactor to Tradescant's Ark.

The early florists were not interested in selling their beloved plants, but in the same way as the continental *fleuristes*, they enjoyed perfecting them and showing them off to each other. They took the quest very seriously, and there were participants who became somewhat obsessive. For some it ended in tears with the fiasco of tulipomania; others continued to select the best specimens for propagation thus instigating the movement which ultimately resulted in the magnificent auriculas we enjoy today. Florists had a particular love of detail: strange, odd petal formations such as doubling, or the hose-in-hose mutation whereby one flower is

PARKINSON'S DESCRIPTIONS OF AURICULAS

The purple Bears eare or Murrey Cowslip with green leaves and a 'whitish ring or circle at the bottome of each flower'.

The murrey Cowslip without eyes.

The Tawney Beares eares with leaves of a 'greater shewe of mealiness'.

The Deepe or bloud red Beares eares with eyes and green leaves.

The Violet coloured Beares eares with somewhat mealy large leaves.

The Spaniards blush Beares eare with larger flowers 'resembling the blush of a Spaniard, whose tawny skin cannot declare so pure a blush as the English can'.

The Scarlet or light red Beares eare with pale green leaves.

The Rose coloured Beares eare with leaf 'a little mealy'.

The Blew Beares eares with Borage leaves (which Parkinson rightly discounts as a real Beares eare).

The great white Beares eare.

The lesser white Beares eare.

The great faire yellow Beares eare with flowers resembling a nosegay (as mentioned above).

The greater yellow Beares eare.

The great Straw coloured Beares eare.

The lesser straw coloured Beares eare.

The lesser yellow Beares eare.

The deepe yellow or Cowslip Beares eare.

The blush Beares eare 'having the ground of the flower of a dark or dunne yellow colour shadowed over a little with a shew of light purple ... the edges of the flower being tipt with a little deeper shew of that purple colour, the bottome of the flower abiding wholly yellow without any circle and is of great beauty'.

The Haire coloured Beares eare, 'the flower is usually of a fine light brown yellow colour, which wee doe usually call Haire colour, and sometimes browner, the edges of the flower have a shew or shadow of light purple or blush about them'.

The yellow variable Beares eare, with an almost flat flower 'dasht about the edges only with purple, being more yellow in the bottome of the flower, then in any other part'.

The variable greene Beares eare without a circle, similar to the last, with 'flowers of a yellowish greene colour more closed than the former, having purplish edges, especially when they have stood blowne some time'.

found within another. They studied their flowers up close and valued the striping, feathering and mottling which occurred, for example when tulips 'broke'. Unusual plants they considered 'miracles of nature'.

Amongst the new and fashionable plants that were sweeping Europe at the end of the sixteenth century there were four which were accorded especial esteem: carnations, tulips, ranunculus and anemones. A short while later the auricula joined the elite club. The *Paradisus* begins with a section entitled 'the Ordering of the Garden of Pleasure', which includes information about the design of the knots and borders fashionable in gardens. Then, 'having thus formed out the garden', Parkinson proceeds to 'furnish the inward parts' with flowers.

Auriculas are mentioned in Chapter IV, the section which deals with 'The nature and names of divers Out-Landish flowers that for their pride, beauty and earlinesse, are to be planted in a Garden of pleasure for delight.' Parkinson says of them: 'Beares Eares or French Cowslips must not want their deserved commendations. Seeing their flowers, being many set together upon a stalke, doe seeme every one of them to be a Nosegay alone and of itself; and besides the many differing colours that are to be seen in them as white, yellow, blush, purple, red, tawney, murrey, hair colour &c which encrease much delight in all sorts of the Gentry of the Land, they are not unfurnished with a pretty sweete sent which doth add an encrease of pleasure in those that make them an ornament for their wearing.'

Starling.

Nosegays were small bunches of scented flowers and herbs which had been in use since Medieval days to keep the nose happy and 'gay' by masking the many unpleasant smells which hung about the streets at the time. Until the eighteenth century it was the custom to wear the nosegay as an ornament rather than to carry it as was fashionable later, especially in the Victorian era. We find this mentioned in the description and illustration of the 'great faire yellow Beares eare' which bears as many as thirty pips 'standing so close together as they seeme to be a Nosegay alone'.

Parkinson in fact details twenty-one types of beares eare and comments that there are many more but that he has 'onely set down those that have come under mine owne view'. His list makes for attractive reading and provides a vivid picture of auriculas of 1629.

In Parkinson's description of the Haire coloured Beares eare, it is tempting to speculate that the suggestion of shadowing or shading about the petals referred to as 'blush' indicates the emergence of something like our modern Alpine. It is hard to confirm or deny, but it is as well to be wary of such speculations, for as Biffen warns, 'descriptions have to be accepted with caution, for when they were written systematic botany was in embryonic condition'. (This is a warning I have found worth bearing in mind at all times when investigating the history of this flower.)

Likewise, could his last two variable auriculas

be early Stripes? Once again it is hard to be sure. The term 'variable' here is a translation of the latin word *versicolor* which *could* mean striped as it indicates something party-coloured, but the fact that the yellow variable bear's ear is 'dashd about *the edges* only' and the variable green bear's ear is of a yellowish green colour 'having purple *edges*', once again implies something different from what we now understand as striping – although possibly it was a development in that direction.

From the sum of these descriptions several things are clear: these plants resemble our border types; they bore both smooth green leaves and mealy leaves of very varied shapes, sizes and edgings; a central white circle or 'eye' was found in some of the flowers; and an improvement in quality had occurred, in that 'the great faire Beares eare' bears a big truss of *thirty* pips.

Seven of these auriculas, plus one 'Beares eare Sanicule', are illustrated by woodcuts, but it is difficult to rely on these illustrations, charming though they are.

Amongst Parkinson's achievements were not only those as an apothecary and a gardener but also as a keen plant collector, listing 125 types of fashionable tulips growing in his garden. Through his gardens and his published work he shared the appreciation of plants which were of no practical use but 'served only to deck up the gardens of the curious.'

THOMAS JOHNSON'S EDITION OF THE *HERBALL*

A second, posthumous edition of Gerard's *Herball* was published in 1633. Thomas Johnson (*c.*1600–1644) was the able young apothecary who got the job of editing it. His chief interest was wild plants, rather than garden plants, and to achieve his ambition to catalogue all the native plants of England he made several plant-hunting trips which resulted in the first accounts of English wild plants.

In the years since the first edition of the *Herball* progress had been made in identification, and in Johnson's vastly improved book he included some

Facing page: Mrs. L. Hearne.

800 new plants and 700 new illustrations. He was far more scientifically-minded than Gerard and dismissed many of the earlier more outlandish and fabulous notions. That being said he did claim that a piece of the root of Damasonium would help 'such as have devoured *lepus marinus* or have been bitten by a toad'. To give him his due however, he is quoting Dioscorides.

The majority of the text regarding auriculas remains as in the first edition. The same number and types of *Auricula ursi* are described, but regarding Gerard's scepticism about the existence of the 'shining red bears ear' Johnson adds the rider, 'Our Author is here without cause injurious to Mattiolus, for he figures and describes onely the common first described yellow Beares eare: yet if he had said the floures were of a light shining red, he had not erred, for I have seen these floures of all the reds both bright and darke that one may imagine.'

There is also an interesting amplification to the section 'The Kindes' which introduces us to some prominent gardeners of the age. After a general introduction of the 'Mountain Cowslips or Beares-eares', Johnson adds the passage, 'The floures some are fairer than othersome, and their colours so various, that it is hard to find words to express them, but they may be referred to as whites, reds, yellows and purples; for of all the varieties and mixtures of these they chiefly consist. The gardens of Mr Tradescant and Mr Tuggie are at this present furnished with great varieties of these flours.'

THE TRADESCANTS

The Tradescants (the father and son were both called John) were the leading British horticulturalists of the day. In 1610 John Tradescant the Elder (1570–1638) went to work for Robert Cecil, the first Earl of Salisbury at Hatfield House in Hertfordshire, and he also visited the Earl's other property at Cranborne in Dorset. He undertook plant-buying excursions all over Europe for these gardens. In Paris he visited the King's gardener Jean Robin. By 1615 he had moved on from Hatfield, and he subsequently supervised several other great gardens before landing the post of

Keeper of his Majesty's Garden, Silkworms and Vines at Oatlands for King Charles I in 1630. He continued to travel and brought back many rarities. His son, John (1608–62) followed in his footsteps, both in plant-hunting and in the appointment as Keeper of the King's Garden.

Their own garden, in the then largely rural Lambeth (Gerard writes of finding a yellow loosetrife 'along the Meadowes as you goe from Lambeth to Battersey neere London') held probably the most extensive plant collection in England, while at their house was a collection of curiosities known as The Ark. This was effectively the first museum open to the public in England, one at which 'a Man might in one daye behold and collecte into one place more Curiosities than hee should see if he spent all his life in Travell'. The contents of The Ark eventually went to Oxford and formed the basis of the Ashmolean museum.

In 1634 John Tradescant the Elder published a catalogue of the 750 plants growing in his garden between 1629 and 1633, in which fourteen *Auricula ursi* are listed. This list, which is published as Appendix I of Prudence Leith-Ross' 1984 book *The Tradescants*, contains fourteen auriculas described mainly by colour, but two of which bear new names: *Holoserico* (silky) and an early mention of what could be a raiser's name, the *Potrine* and *altera Potrine*. Could these refer to the *Poutrain* bear's ear mentioned by Franeau?

We also find an *albo & rubro variegata* (white and red mixed) and an *albo & Purpureo variegata* (white and purple mixed), but as no English translation was made at the time, the use of the term '*variegata*' does not offer any firm confirmation to the striping question. Interestingly though, Leith-Ross' Appendix does give the modern (1980s) botanical names, and of the fourteen *Auricula ursi* only four – the white coloured bear's ear, the greatest yellow bear's ear, the smooth leaved bear's ear and the middle yellow bear's ear – are credited with being *Primula auricula* L. The rest are listed as *Primula x pubescens* Jacq.

John Tradecant the Younger published a fuller catalogue in 1656, which included the contents of The Ark as well as the plants, under the title *Musaeum Tradescantianum or A Collection of RARITIES preserved at South Lambeth neer London.*

This catalogue contains the same auriculas, but a seventeenth century translation *is* offered, which does cast light on the striping question. *Auricula ursi Albo & rubro variegata* is here translated as '*striped* white and red Beares eares', the first actual use of the term 'striped'. Puzzlingly however, *A.u. Albo & purpureo variegata*' is rendered as 'party-coloured and purple Beares eares' without mention of either white or striping, thus implying that these terms were still imprecise.

Once again in modern botanical taxonomy only the same four are credited with being *Primula auricula*. Amongst the remainder we find that the red bear's ear was thought (by John Harvey who helped to compile the modern botanical list) possibly to be *Primula integrifolia* L. and the violet coloured bear's ear, *P. halleri* Honck. This endorses the remainder of the previous quotation from Biffen, 'descriptions have to be accepted with caution, for when they were written systematic botany was in embryonic condition and the lines of demarcation between Auriculas and other species of Primula were not defined.'

The fact that the Tradescants' names were, in Gerard, linked with Mr Tuggie, well known as a nurseryman, together with the large number of plants on this list, have led to speculation that the Tradescants also sold plants. However, although they had enough land, no accounts of plant sales have ever been found. C. Oscar Moreton however, does suggest that Tradescant, 'through his improvement of the flower, was able to supply the Dutch florist with an endless variety of new sorts'. Mr Tuggie is Ralph Tuggy (or Toogy, Toogey or Tuggye – spelling at the time had not been standardized) who lived and gardened in Westminster. He *is* thought to be one of the first nurserymen-florists in the city. Tuggy was also known to Parkinson, who called him 'the most industrious preserver of nature's beauties'.

Ralph and his wife Catherine had nine children, all of whom were christened at St Margaret's Westminster. Johnson indicates that Ralph had already died by 1633 as, when referring to gilly-flowers, he urges readers to 'repair to the garden of Mistress Tuggie (the wife of my late deceased friend Mr Ralph Tuggie) in Westminster which in the excellencie and variety of these delights exceedeth all that I have seen'. The exact whereabouts of the garden is not known, but one of Tuggy's sons, Richard, subsequently became a herbalist. We know this because in 1658, by which time Ralph had been dead for many years, scribbled on the flyleaf of a catalogue of the Oxford Botanical Garden, the curator Jacob Bobart the Elder (1599–1679) noted, 'Tuggee in Westminster beyond ye Abbey, *Lotus arbor, cyclamen vernum*'. Thus it is likely that Richard followed in his father's footsteps.

PARKINSON'S *THEATRUM BOTANICUM: A GARDEN OF SIMPLES*

Parkinson's *Paradisus* had clearly been aimed at the gardener rather than the physician, but in 1640 he produced a second work, *Theatrum Botanicum*, subtitled *A Garden of Simples*, which is effectively one of the last herbals. In this however, Parkinson amplifies his descriptions of auriculas, especially the ones not discussed in the *Paridisus*. He mentions them by colour and gives attention to the form of the leaves, and it is here we find the first mention of a Double: 'The double purple hath the purple flower once more double than the single, but is not constant'.

Here too we find confirmation that the term 'stript' is now in more general usage, something confirmed by comparison with other flowers: 'The stript purple differs in leafe little or nothing, from the ordinary purple, nor yet in flower, but onely that it is variously stript with a kinde of whitish blush colour; some of these will change wholly into one or other colour, as all or most of the severall sorts of stript flowers whether Tulipas, Gilliflowers are observed often to doe, yet as in them so in these, if they change to the deeper colour they seldom or never returnee to be marked, as they will if they change into lighter.' There is also a 'party-coloured red and white', which could also be a Stripe, but Parkinson adds that he had not seen it. We can thus feel more confident that something resembling what we would call a Stripe had arrived by this date.

Parkinson also mentions 'sundry sorts of blushes' and comments that new colours arise every year from sowing seeds, some better than others. It would also appear that some of the whites may 'be set under the blushes and other paler sorts', indicating that the colours are exhibiting a greater degree of subtlety. There are some entirely new colours 'the heavens blue' and a 'paler blew'. The yellows are the most numerous, 'so mixed and varied thereon that I cannot express them' and range from 'lemman', through straw coloured to shamwey (chamois).We also find the '*Poutrine* or blood red', possibly the *Poutrain* of Franeau or the *Potrine* of Gerard, together with some entirely new names which show a development from simple colour names: 'the dainty violet *Collie* as the French call it or *farre Collier* we in English', and the similarly coloured *Cambersine*. Parkinson also distinguishes the leathercoats with 'large mealy leaves' and makes the point that 'many of them will flower twice in the year ... if the Autumn prove temperate and moist'.

BREEDING STARTS TO BECOME SELECTIVE

From Parkinson's account we get the impression that by 1640 there are almost too many types of auricula available to enumerate them in the way of the old herbals. So popular were these flowers that an increasing number of people were growing plants and selling them to satisfy the need felt by the florists. At this stage most were grown from seed, and each batch produced very varying specimens resulting in a huge variety. It was becoming apparent however, that discrimination was necessary if truly spectacular plants were to result, and so breeding began to become somewhat more selective. By the time the auriculas joined the carnation, tulip, anemone and ranunculus as the most desired flowers, the aims of the florist had become more specific. By the time the hyacinth, the polyanthus and the pink joined the select band and formed the eight classic florists' flowers, 'improvement' had become the name of the game.

To some people the idea of interfering with nature in order to perfect flowers was not acceptable. In *Descriptions of England* published in 1587 William Harrison had written: 'How art also helpeth nature in the daily colouring, doubling, and enlarging the proportion of our flowers, it is incredible to report: for so curious and cunning are our gardeners now in these days that they presume to do what they like with nature.'

This sentiment was echoed in Andrew Marvell's 1681 poem 'The Mower against Gardens', where the image of man tampering with nature is used as a metaphor for the deterioration of society.

With strange perfumes he did the Roses taint,
And flow'rs themselves were taught to paint
The Tulip, white, did for complexion seek;
and learn'd to interline its cheek ...
... .Till all enforc'd; the Fountain and the Grot
While the sweet fields do lie forgot ...

THE FLORISTS' FEAST

The florists, unconcerned, delighted in their blooms and continued their quest for perfection. They were in the main, people from the more comfortable, leisured echelons of society. They were gregarious, and from the outset they combined the admiration of their flowers with having a good time.

As early as May 1631 there was a report of a florists' feast being held at Norwich. In the course of the event the guests were entertained by a play entitled *Rhodon and Iris* by Ralph Knevet, a 'remote scion of the great Norfolk family of Knyvett'. The play, a heroic and romantic pastoral in the style of Spencer in which the characters were flowers, was prefaced by an address to the author's 'much respected friends of the Society of Florists', declaring that the feast is 'celebrated by such a conflux of Gentlemen of birth and quality in whose presence (I thinke) your cities welfare partly consists'. The pastoral was dedicated to Nicholas Bacon of Gillingham who was apparently 'fervently addicted to a speculation of the virtues and beauties of all flowers'.

Facing page: Chorister.

Old Red Dusty Miller.

It is not known if flowers were exhibited at this event – this first recorded feast may simply have been a social gathering of business people and flower-lovers of the town. The feast however, angered the Norwich Puritans who disapproved of all theatrical performances but had a special loathing of any which celebrated Flora, goddess of flowers, in their view a pagan deity.

Running beneath this, however, was the deep antipathy Puritans felt towards the Catholic Queen Henrietta Maria, who was almost the physical embodiment of all that they particularly disliked. Henrietta Maria, daughter of the King of France, had been married by proxy to Charles I at the age of fifteen. John Tradescant had actually been at the service in Paris, assisting Lord Buckingham, the King's favourite, with his voluminous luggage, which contained twenty-seven suits – one in white velvet entirely set with diamonds. Buckingham stood proxy for the King at the lavish ceremony in Notre Dame and then accompanied the young queen back to England together with her retinue, including a bishop and twenty-eight Catholic priests – hardly calculated to inspire the confidence of the Puritans, or indeed the population.

Henrietta Maria was a fervent flower-lover. She had grown up in pleasure gardens with magical grottoes and fountains. She found nothing similar in England, although Parkinson, in dedicating the *Paradisus* to her, 'Knowing your Majestie so much delighted with all the faire Flowers of a Garden and furnished with them as farre beyond others you are eminent before them', did offer her this volume as his own 'Garden of Pleasant Flowers' and so gained her friendship and entry into her circle and her gardens.

To the Puritans it was bad enough that she was a Catholic and a 'worshipper of Flora', but the fact that she adored plays, pastorals and masques irritated them even more intensely, as they considered theatrical performances the works of the devil. Both King Charles I and Henrietta Maria were addicted to court masques, not only as spectators but as performers. In 1624, just before her marriage, the Queen had danced in Anne of Austria's *Ballet de la Reine, dansé par les nymphes du jardin* [Ballet of the Queen danced by the garden nymphs].

Then in 1626, as Queen Consort to the King of England, she wrote and acted in *The Queen's Masque*. A Queen on stage! The Puritans, and quite a number of other people, considered this outrageous, and the event caused no little controversy. 'I have not much honor of The Quene's Masque', reported Henry Manners, 'For if they were not all, soome were in men's apparel.'

In February 1631, just prior to the first florist's feast in Norwich, Queen Henrietta Maria took the role of Chloris in Ben Jonson's masque *Chloridia*. In this, as in Botticelli's painting *Primavera*, Chloris is transformed by Juno into Flora, the goddess of flowers. As with many of these masques it contained a political subtext – usually relating to the glorification of the royal couple, but this time also symbolizing the granting of the Divine Right to the Queen. This, of course enraged the Puritans, and the following year a lawyer, William Prynne, published *Histrio-Mastix,* an attack on the theatre, in which women actors were referred to a 'notorious whores' and 'whorishly impudent'. This barely-veiled attack on the Queen was considered intolerable by the King, and he had Prynne arrested. He was then tried, disbarred and expelled from Lincoln's Inn, stripped of his degree, fined £5000, imprisoned at the King's pleasure, pilloried, had his ears cropped – and later his cheek was branded with the letters S.L. for 'seditious libell'.

Facing page: Sandwood Bay.

William Strode, chaplain to the Bishop of Norwich, wrote a poem, 'A Prologe crown'd with Flowers On the Florists Feast at Norwich', which he hoped would be conciliatory, but at the end he did chide the critics:

To them that cry
Our Stage doth savour of lewd Vanity
To frighten tender mindes with jealous feares
I wish true Sense.

Another poem, written over a decade later in 1645 by Mathew Stevenson, 'At the Florists feast at Norwich. Flora wearing a crown', seems to indicate that there had been an interruption to the annual feasts, as in the poem Flora thanks the company, saying without them she would have no feast, but continues, 'How have I been neglected of late yeares'. This implies further trouble resulted in cancellations, 'since the seeds of discord I am overgrown with weed'.

The poem does, however, leave us in no doubt that the feast was a jolly, boozy sort of event, just the sort of which the Puritans so strongly disapproved:

And the best brewer sent us in our bere
Since thenere neither wants Beer, wine nor guest
Flaggons and flowers shall flow at Floras feast.
Let chearly Cups a carowsing day.

This is a strange poem but significant in the history of florists' flowers. It reinforces the view that florists were only interested in selected flowers. Flora here says that the feast is not for 'rustic fopperies' nor even for the lily and the rose, 'though of flowers the King and Queen'. Another part of the poem then sets out the names of the flowers which would be present in a list, which contains many italicized words that seem to make little sense until one realizes that they are in fact the names of early cultivars. At first thought to be the fashionable tulips, it was later found that many refer to carnations which can be found in John Rea's *Flora.*

Facing page: Wye Hen.

CHAPTER 5

A Comfort in Troubled Times

Throughout history the development of this plant attracted the attention of interesting men and women who loved and nurtured it, and who also wrote about it. A number of them were associated with the Oxford botanic garden, and their books are preserved at the Oxford University library, where we will follow the trail of evidence.

John Rea (d. 1681), a well-known florist, offers us some interesting clues in the development of the auricula. We know only that he was a well-esteemed horticulturalist, that he lived at Kinlet, a village at the north of the Wyre Valley in Worcestershire, that he had a daughter called Minerva, that he was a very experienced gardener ('Fourty years are now completed since I began to be a Planter') and that he had lived through the troubled times of the Civil War, Commonwealth and Restoration.

Beyond that we only have his book, *Flora, Ceres & Pomona: seu De Florum Cultura or a Complete Florilege, furnished with all the requisites belonging to a florist*, which he published in 1665, with a second edition in 1676 and a third after his death in 1702. It gives us a very good picture of contemporary gardens, as it contains an illuminating section on garden design and planning. One of the dedicatees is Lord Gerard of Gerard's Bromley, whose garden Rea is thought to have laid out. The book is also full of practical advice and deals with planting, maintenance and tools, as well as plants including flowers, shrubs and trees with special emphasis on fruit trees.

Rea's personality shines through his writing, linking us immediately to a fellow gardener and through him to a network of other gardeners and growers. One of the dedicatees is Sir Thomas Hanmer, whose important contribution to auricula history we shall look at shortly and who Rea credits with being the inspiration for this book. The second edition also contains a dedication to Lady Hanmer in the form of a charming poem which yet again makes use of the conceit of the book's 'preserving' the flowers to be enjoyed in winter.

To Lady Hanmer
Madam, If you but deign to look
Upon this plain but Flowery book
All there inscrib'd you soon will know
Since in your gardens they do grow
And though you were no Florist bred
Yet to a Florist married,
But when Winter draweth on
And all these Beauties are quite gone
That you no more on them can look
You'll find them in this Flowery book.

The subject of Rea's *Flora* is not the grand garden but the newer, middle-ranking type which was then becoming more commonplace. Rea has no time for pretension: 'Noble fountains, grottoes, statues &c are excellent ornaments and marks of magnificence; so all such dead works in gardens, ill done, are little better than blocks in the way to interrupt sight but not at all to satisfy the understanding. A choice collection of living beauties, rare plants, flowers and fruit are indeed the wealth glory and delight of a garden'. Amongst these 'living beauties' is the auricula, which Rea discusses at some length.

In the second edition Rea adds that he received

Facing page: Susannah.

AURICULAS IN REA'S *FLORA*

Beares Eares, are a nobler kinds of cowslips, and much esteemed, in respect of the many excellent varieties there of late years discovered, differing in the size, fashion, and colour of the green leaves as well as the flowers which we will list under these colours, namely purple, red or scarlet, yellow or Buff colour, Snow or milk-white.'

(First he considers the purples)

The purple ... commonly called the fair Downham ... takes its name from my good friend *Mr John Downham* a reverent Divine, and an industrious *Florist.*

Mr Good's purple Auricula a strong plant ... with snow white eyes which will not wash with rain ... This noble kind was raised by *Mr Austen* in *Oxford* and given to *Mr John Good* of *Balliol College*, whose now it is there called.

Mistris Buggs her fine purple was raised by her in Battersey neer London.

Mr Whitmore's purple Purple Fransway, beareth great tufts of shining purple flowers with very large white eyes.

Rickets sable Auricula raised by Mr Rickets of Hogsden often remembered the best and most faithful Florist now about London.

The purple striped Auricula small weak low stalk bearing four or five purple flowers striped in white.

The purple and Lemon-coloured striped Auricula bigger longer than the last, eight to ten flowers, Lemon coloured striped with reddish purple; this was also raised by *Mistris Buggs* before mentioned and is a flower of good esteem.'

(Next he turns to the reds)

One of the best I know is called *Mistris Austins scarlet*, great tufts of fine scarlet flowers has been raised in Oxford by Mr Jacob Bobart keeper of the Publick Garden. Other divers sorts of reds upon many of which several fantastical names (by those that raised them) have been imposed such as the *fair Virgin, the Matron, the Alderman, Mercury and other Planets, the Cow, the Red Bull* etc.

(He has no love of yellows)

The yellow Auricula is of small esteem ... more ordinary sorts are commonly cast away.

(Nor are whites much liked)

White also of small variety and esteem the best is that called *the Virgins milk* hath large mealy leaves ... great tufts of milk-white flowers with snow white eyes which placed among the purples, sets off and adds to their glory.

(And finally ...)

Every Florist has his *Leather-Coat* many of which yet remain and retain the names of those that raised them as Tradescants Leathercoat, Lances, Tugies, Turners, Colins, Looker, Humphries, Meracows, Mows, Mullares, Randolls, and I.

a plant the previous spring from his 'worthy friend William Whitmore of Balmes near Hodgsen, Esquire, the *Black Imperial,* small leaves and short stalks but beareth many fair flowers close set together of so dark a purple colour, that without much error it may be called black with fair snow white eyes: this was raised in *Oxford.*'

Thus we have not only the purple and lemon Stripe and the weak purple Stripe, but we learn that by this time there has also been another development – this purple stripe, small and weak though it is, 'of this sort and colour *we have one which beareth double flowers*'. A Double Stripe has thus appeared.

In this second edition he also adds many more reds: 'Crimson, Carnation and one that beareth great tufts of blood-red flowers with fair white eyes' and 'infinite other varieties of Rose-colours, Blushes, Cinnamon and other fine colours ... with white eyes which will not wash'.

As well as indicating that considerable

Facing page: Joan Elliott.

Glen Elg.

development has taken place, Rea's book also affords us a fascinating glimpse of the people involved in raising auriculas. A dozen established auricula growers are named, and probably they all knew, or at least knew of, each other. It is worth noting that there were also women growing good auriculas: Mistris Buggs and Mistris Austin were obviously active in the auricula world.

Further, although it had been usual to name a new auricula variety after the raiser, things were changing. Mr Good's purple Auricula was in fact raised by Mr Austen, and Mistris Austin's Scarlet was raised by Mr Jacob Bobart. Importantly, Rea also points out that it is becoming fashionable for 'fantastical names' such as 'Mercury (and other planets)' to be 'imposed on' the plants by the grower – so by 1665 we are seeing the beginning of cultivar names.

As to the actual plants, when describing Mr Good's purple auricula Rea comments that it has 'snow white eyes which will not wash with rain', which implies an awareness of the presence of paste on other sorts. Is this perhaps the beginning of the distinction between the Self with its ring of farina and an Alpine type without? We see also that the diversity of colour both in flowers and leaves is valued, and we learn that there were some attractive stripes and even the Double Stripe. Yellows (probably because most numerous) and whites were poorly regarded.

Having described the plants Rea continues with instructions for their culture. It is interesting that he begins by saying, 'The best sorts of Auriculas are set in pots, which they will well deserve'. He continues, 'Place in sun all winter with Glasses, defend them from over much wet but do not house them they will do better in the open air'. He also mentions growing them in borders together with a variety of old-fashioned flowers.

OXFORD AND THE BOBARTS

In referring to auriculas, Rea makes several references to Oxford, because a little hub of enthusiasts were congregated around the botanic garden. In 1621 Lord Danby, who in his youth had been page to Sir Philip Sidney, established the first botanic garden in England in the city of Oxford. As with most such botanic gardens it was not created with florists in mind but was planted with 'divers simples for the faculty of medicine'.

The first Keeper or *Hortus Praefectus* was in fact John Tradescant the Elder, but he died after a year, and the post went to a German from Brunswick, Jacob Bobart, known as Bobart the Elder, as he had a son, another Jacob, who even as a young man was very keen on botany. Young Jacob worked with his father in the garden and eventually took over as *Hortus Praefectus* himself. He also gave lectures on botany, although his status was never defined. Between them they left a very important legacy by way of catalogues and herbaria. Herbaria, collections of dried plants, have always had a special value in that they prove indisputably that the plants they contain were actually germinated, propagated and cultivated in certain places at specific times.

A Visit to Oxford

Knowing that the Bobart records contained material about auriculas, I made my way to Oxford one crisp winter's day, eager to see them with my own eyes. Dr Stephen Harris, the Druce Curator of

Facing page: Nocturne.

Oxford University Herbaria, welcomed me into a business-like little room where portraits of past botanists including Linnaeus gazed down on us. He had set out a number of interesting old volumes.

Bobart the Elder's Catalogue and Hortus Siccus

First came a small book, the *Catalogus Plantarum*, in which Jacob Bobart the Elder had listed all the plants growing in the Oxford Botanic Garden in 1648. It contained six auriculas named in Latin with translation:

AURICULAS IN BOBART THE ELDER'S *CATALOGUS*	
Auricula ursi flo. albo	White Flow'd Beares ear
A. u. rubete	Red Beares ear
A. u. purp var.	Purple striped Beares ear
A. u. sulph	Brimstone Beares ear
A. u. purp	Purple Beares ear
A. u. caeruleo	Blew Beares ear

The *Catalogus* dates from some twenty years before John Rea's *Flora*, so I was not surprised that the plants did not bear any 'fantastical' or even grower's names.

The second book which I was shown was compiled ten years later by Stephens and Browne with the help of Bobart the Younger, who was only fifteen years old at the time. The section on auriculas began with a short description. 'Small and large flowers which can be pale or darker; leaves narrowly dentate, green and whitish and mealy resembling a bear's ear. Many elegant varieties and many different colours and forms, stem pendant and producing lots of seed'.

Having shown me these printed catalogues, Dr Harris then produced the first of the herbaria, the *Hortus Siccus* of Jacob Bobart the Elder. It was a small leather-bound book with 2584 specimens glued into 297 pages.

1648 CATALOGUE (STEPHENS AND BROWNE WITH BOBART THE YOUNGER)	
Nine auriculas are listed, some with an indication of the provenance: G for Gerard, P for Parkinson, Clusius, and Jean Robin's *Catalogus Parisiensis*	
Auricula ursi major flore albo	G. 787 P 238 Great white Beares ear
A. u. fl. purp.	Purple Beares ear
A. u. fl. purp. caeruleo	Violet Beares ear
A. u. fl. rubella P. G. quartus Clusius	Great Scarlet Beares ear
A. u. fl. rubio P. G. 2 Clusius	Great Red Beares ear
A. u. flor taneto P. G.	Tawny Beares ear
A. u. flore purp. vareigata	*Cat Parisiensis* Striped Beares ear
A. u. flore luteo G flavo. P.	Cowslip Beares ear
A. u. crinis coloris	Haire coloured Beares ear

I asked how old it was. 'It is difficult to date,' Dr Harris replied. 'It disappeared for years and ended up in the Bedford Medical Library before being returned to Oxford. There are three sets of handwriting at work in it, the two Bobarts and John Ray (who died in 1705), so it was evidently put together over several years. There's a note on the back cover saying that in 1687 there were 2577 plants in it.'

We found all the auriculas on page 33. They were attractively set out, and for me it was rather moving to see for the first time the ghosts of these flowers which had been growing over 300 years ago. There were eleven pressed as complete specimens with stems. At the top of the page, in the elegant hand of Jacob Bobart the Elder, was written, '*Auricula ursi variorum colore* – Beares ears of divers colours'. The colours, tones of reds and yellows, were still quite bright, and traces of paste were visible. With the exception of one plant which only had two pips, they averaged about eight pips per truss. One plant had leaves and tiny roots.

Beneath these came a series of single pips, most with descriptions and some with names, including some 'fantastical' or cultivar, names: 'Plumpton', a stripe; 'Duchess of Cleaveland', a small yellow; 'Flourishing Prince', a stripe; 'Fair Hanna', a yellow; 'Buggs', purple and yellow; 'Rodses Moraston', double; 'Luckers', purple and cream stripe. There was also a double purple, a haire colour, a buff and a yellow (both stripes).

Bobart the Younger's Hortus Siccus

Next came the *Hortus Siccus* of Jacob Bobart the Younger, which was made up of single sheets. 'The dating of this also remains difficult, but it was probably created early in the career of Bobart the Younger,' Dr Harris said. 'A manuscript note dated 24th November 1666 is pinned on one of Bobart's notebooks, which has led to this being cited as the date, although there is no indication in the notebook to what that date refers, and the indices don't help either as they are written on paper which dates from the time of George III, which is after Bobart's death.'

When I said how miraculous it was that such fragile things have survived at all, Dr Harris agreed, saying nevertheless some items had not fared so well. In the nineteenth century part of the Herbarium archive was sold off as wastepaper to shopkeepers in Oxford, and during the last war papers recording the planting of the botanic garden were used as fuel by the then Keeper in an effort to keep the hothouses going. It failed – the plants died anyway.

The *Hortus Siccus* of Bobart the Younger consists of 2202 specimens on these loose sheets which are stored in sixteen boxes. Originally they were bound together as books and stored at the botanic garden. 'Why they were cut up is not clear', said Dr Harris. 'But after being "hidden" for three centuries within the Oxford University Herbaria they have now been catalogued to put online.'

Most of the plants were grown in or near the botanic gardens – but not all. There is a marine algae *Fucus Serratus* clearly not from this area. Nor is it true that the *Hortus Siccus* was made up

only of the Bobarts' horticultural failures. Many of the specimens had obviously grown well. Most importantly it shows that the botanic garden was not just a collection of medicinal plants. From the contents – narcissi, hyacinths, anemones and auriculas – it was clearly rich in the ornamentals of the day.

The handwriting in this *Hortus Siccus*, Dr Harris explained, was that of Humphrey Sibthorpe (1713–97), a rather disappointing Sherardian Professor who gave only one lecture and published nothing in his forty-year tenure and who, as we shall see, was rather unpleasant to the artist Georg Dionysius Ehret (a very talented artist about whom we will hear a lot more in due course).

We see three very good specimens of striped bears ears: a purple with a truss of sixteen pips, a '*Sanicula alpine sive Auricula ursi*' or yellow bear's ear together with four unnamed auriculas: a dark red, a yellow, a yellowy-green and a deep purple, possibly striped. Two of the specimens have roots and are thought to have been grown in the Badminton garden of the Duchess of Beaufort (of whom we shall also hear more shortly). Bobart the Younger apparently sent seed to her gardener and visited her garden in 1693.

The Sherardian and Du Bois Herbariums

Next Dr Harris produced the *Sherardian Herbarium* which consists of approximately 12,000 specimens dating from 1680–1796. This also contained auriculas, and I saw a page with five specimens which bore between two and nine pips: an amber coloured Stripe, a mauve and yellow Stripe with a clear eye, a yellow, a deeper amber coloured Double and a deeper reddish purple. Its creator, William Sherard (1659–1728) was a talented botanist who, as we shall see, worked as a young man for the auricula-loving Duchess of Beaufort. He later became British Consul in Smyrna from where he collected many plants before founding the Chair of Botany at Oxford.

There was yet more to come. Dr Harris next got out the *Du Bois Herbarium* which contained another four specimens. There were two yellows with very big leaves. Then there was an excellent and very large black specimen with a pale eye, leaves and roots labelled *Auricula ursi mango atropurpereo bone candido*. Could this magnificent specimen, I wondered, be the *Black Imperial* mentioned by Rea as 'being raised in Oxford'? And finally was another yellow, and these last two were labelled as coming from 'Mr Stonestreet', the Rev. William Stonestreet who died in 1716.

I left the Department of Plant Science, my head full of these plants from the past, and set off to visit the botanic garden, site of so many of the Bobarts' activities. Walking through Oxford's cobbled streets, the past seemed to envelop me and as I entered the garden I could easily imagine father and son working there together.

I had read that Bobart the Elder was considered eccentric, and one of the reasons cited was that he liked to garden with his pet goat beside him. Although goats and gardens seem incompatible (unless for controlled weed disposal) I had rather enjoyed imagining this scene. Dr Harris, however, had disabused me of such reveries, saying that this idea probably derived from a prose poem, *Vertumnus* written 1713 which depicted Bobart on the cover. On the way to the garden I had found a copy of this picture in a book, *British Botanists* by John Gilmour published in 1946, which I picked up in a second-hand bookshop. There was Jacob Bobart with his long beard (which apparently he 'had a fancy to tagg … with silver which brought much company into the garden') wearing a flared frock coat and holding the snake-entwined staff of the healer. He is standing in front of the entrance to the garden, a dog sleeping in the background and, yes, a goat is gazing up at him rather expectantly … possibly as a symbol of wisdom rather than a weeding aid. The poem it illustrated is by Evans and was written to celebrate the *Hortus Siccus*. One verse runs:

Their Barks, or Roots, their Flow'rs or Leaves
Thy HORTUS SICCUS still receives:
In Tomes twice Ten, that Work immense!
With utmost Diligence amass'd
And shall as many Ages last.

Sitting reading these lines in the garden I was pleased to think that the importance of these collections was recognized even then. My mind turned again to the little coterie of people mentioned by Rea. Did Bobart the Elder hold court here in the garden? Did he offer favoured friends auriculas of his own raising? Were Mr and Mistris Austen meanwhile achieving good results with theirs? They passed one of these to Mr John Good (Tutor Good) of Balliol, who liked it so much that he gave it his name.

THE ROYAL SOCIETY

Once again I was amazed at the amount of history encapsulated in this small flower and the number of interesting men and women of the past who nurtured and developed it. These people were all, in their minor ways, part of the movement which was advancing scientific investigation.

As early as 1645 an 'Invisible College' of philosophers established in London what was eventually to become The Royal Society for the Improvement of Natural Knowledge, later known as The Royal Society. This collection of 'ingenious and curious gentlemen' from many disciplines included John Evelyn, Christopher Wren, Samuel Pepys, John Dryden and Robert Boyle. They met to discuss a wide range of scientific matters, paying a subscription of a shilling a week. After the Restoration these great minds were of enormous benefit in rebuilding a country which had been brought low by two Anglo-Dutch wars, a Great Plague in which 68,000 Londoners died and a Great Fire which destroyed much of the capital.

Meanwhile other universities were establishing their own Physik gardens. That of my own *alma mater*, Trinity College Dublin began modestly in 1687 when part of the old kitchen garden was taken over and the gardener was paid an extra 20 shillings a quarter for looking after the new beds. A weeding woman, Margaret Armstrong, was also employed at ten pence a day, her work to include ditch mending. When James I occupied the college between 1689 and 1690 the work of the botanic garden was interrupted. It resumed

Facing page: Winifred.

Marigold.

in 1701 when the first Professor of Medicine, Thomas Molyneux, was installed, and at this stage a new site was chosen near the Anatomy Theatre.

An interesting handwritten catalogue of the plants in this Dublin garden, which is now at the library of the Natural History Museum, London, includes *Auricularum ursi numerous varietas insignis* (numerous remarkable varieties of bear's ears). It is a little volume which has passed through many famous hands. It bears the library stamp of Joseph Banks, but was apparently sent by Dr William Stephens of Dublin (who wrote the second half of it) to Philip Miller, who gave it the Botanical Society of London (which recorded in its minutes that it contains 'several plants not growing in the London Gardens'). Over the next few years, however, the Dublin garden deteriorated. It was invaded by rats searching for offal from the anatomy dissections and eventually only one fig tree and an ancient gardener remained. The garden moved to Ballsbridge in 1806 where it remained for the next hundred years, becoming one of the finest in europe.

SIR THOMAS HANMER, ROYALIST

Sir Thomas Hanmer (1612–78) is one of the most attractive characters involved in the history of the auricula. It was he who inspired John Rea's book, 'For had not your happy Acquaintance reanimated my drooping endeavours in this delight, and your own bounty furnished me with many noble and new Varieties ... ' wrote Rea in the dedication. It was even suggested in the nineteenth century by Lord John Hanmer, one of Sir Thomas's descendants, that plants from Sir Thomas's garden at Bettisfield might have been given to Rea for description in his *Flora*. Whether this was so or not, the two men owned many plants in common. Rea in fact referred to Sir Thomas's collection of plants as 'incomparable' and his judgment in garden matters 'transcendent'.

Sir Thomas imported and raised a superlative tulip, 'Agate Hanmer', of which he was justly proud and to which we find several references in garden literature. Rea, whose favourite flower by far was the tulip, describes it as 'a beautiful flower of three good colours, pale grideline, deep scarlet and pure white, commonly well parted, striped and agated and excellently placed.' Another specimen was sent to John Evelyn who received it in a parcel of flowers sent in 1671. Yet another recipient was the Roundhead General Lambert, who received, via John Rose, a 'great mother root' of this treasure. John Rose (1619–1677) was an eminent nurseryman who had studied under Le Nôtre in France before becoming gardener to the King. He is immortalized in a painting by Hendrick Dankerts which shows him presenting the first pineapple grown in England to Charles II.

The transaction between Sir Thomas and General Lambert proved how little politics matters to plant lovers, for Sir Thomas was a staunch Royalist. In fact his comprehensive collection of plants was amassed and cultivated at Bettisfield, his estate in Flintshire, during the Interregnum, a period when as a Cavalier, he found it politically prudent to stay far from London and keep a low profile.

Facing page: Lee Paul.

For these were still years fraught with political conflict. Sir Thomas came from a distinguished family descended from Welsh Kings, and although his father was a leader of the Puritan party, at the age of twelve he became a cup bearer at the Court of Charles I, and before he was nineteen he had married the beautiful heiress Mistress Elizabeth Baker, one of Queen Henrietta Maria's Maids of Honour. When in 1629, the same year as the *Paradisus* was published, the King dismissed Parliament and begun his Personal Rule, neither he nor his young courtier could have dreamed that he was embarking on a course which would end with his royal head on the block.

Leading up to this however, were years of unrest and finally Civil War during which the 'trusty and well beloved Sir Thomas Hanmer' received a commission in the Royalist army to raise a band of 'Saggitarios' (archers) for use in possible siege situations, something punishable by death if discovered by the Parliamentarians. It is not recorded that Sir Thomas actually fought, but Johnson, the editor of the 1633 edition of Gerard's *Herbal* who also fought on the Royalist side, died from a shot wound incurred at the defence of Basing House.

Not long afterwards Sir Thomas' lands were sequestered, and he and Elizabeth and their two children left the country for France. Sir Thomas did make several clandestine journeys back to England where he lived in various 'hide-outs' or was sheltered by friends. Not long afterwards, however, Elizabeth died in Paris, and her husband put their young son in seminary in Lisbon and left his daughter Trever, then about eight years old, in the care of a Huguenot family and quickly returned to England. He lay low for a while at Hengrave Hall in Suffolk where he met and equally swiftly married another beauty, Mistress Susan Hervey.

They returned to France and lived simply until, on payment of a hefty fine, permission was obtained from Parliament to return home. At first they stayed with Sir Thomas's mother at her Dower House in Halghton, and it was at this period that Sir Thomas began to plan what he would do in his garden when he got back to his own estate at Bettisfield. It is thought likely that Lady Susan was also interested in gardening, as according to Jenny Robinson (to whom I am indebted for much of this information) she certainly had a say in which plants were brought over from Halghton, and her portrait was later painted depicting her holding a copy of the *Paradisus* in her hand.

Many Royalists had been forced to flee abroad, and their great estates, including Theobalds, the great Cecil house where Gerard had gardened, had been taken over by the Parliamentarians.

Abraham Cowley (1618–67) a gifted and precocious poet (he had already written a successful play by the age of ten) was caught up in these troubles. He grew up to become a confidante of the King and Queen, and after the battle of Marston Moor he followed the Queen into exile and spent the next twelve years carrying messages between the royal couple and acting as a spy on their behalf. After the Restoration he returned to England and as well as writing, he too became involved with the founding of the Royal Society.

In 1663 Cowley wrote a long poem 'Six Books of Flowers', which is of interest in that it mirrors the changing attitude to plants. Much of it is a coded celebration of the Restoration; we see the return of Flora and 'God-like Charles and all his peaceful train' who will 'heal the wounds of twenty years' and find them welcomed by flowers, one species of which Flora will choose to be her Vice-Goddess.

The Auricula makes its appeal to Flora, saying:

Great Queen of Flow'rs why is thy snowy Breast
With such a sight of various Posies drest!
Whereas one stalk of mine
Alone a Nosegay is, alone can make thee fine;
A lovely harmless Monster I
Gorgon's many heads outvie.

Cowley however, does seem to approve of the common name by which the plant was known:

Impudent Fool! that first stil'd beauteous flowers
By a detested Name, the Ears of Bears
Worthy himself of Asses Ears a pair
Fairer than Midas once was said to wear.

Sir Thomas's *Garden Book*

We cannot know whether Sir Thomas ever read Cowley's verse, but he, in common with others who lived in the more remote corners of the country, was able to retire quietly to his estates during the dangerous interregnum period. In Sir Thomas' case the enforced leisure was no hardship; it gave him time with his family and his beloved flowers and even more importantly for this story, the opportunity to write his *Garden Book,* a volume which gives us an unrivalled insight into a seventeenth century gentleman's garden, although it was not published until 1933. It also contains information about gardening techniques and clear descriptions of individual plants, but what makes it such a delight is the warmth and joy with which Sir Thomas writes about his plants. His love and enthusiasm for them comes leaping across the centuries.

He grew a great selection of plants: all the florist's flowers, newly imported 'strangers', old-fashioned (even then) traditional cottage-garden flowers, fruit trees and vines. Although tulips were his favourites, he obviously had an extremely soft spot for his Bear's Ears. One can imagine what a balm it was for him and other growers to quietly care for their auriculas throughout these troubled times.

He tells us that, 'In the border under the north wall are beares eares and cowslips; some of the beares eares are marked that came from Rose and Tom Turner, those from Rose last are set by the corner next to the court wall, by the duke cherry. One *faire Frances,* two *purple Frances,* one *redbud,* four *roses olive,* five *Yeomen of Kent,* six *Virgin's gift.*'

Later he gives us this fine description: 'This flower is a kind of Cowslip. Agreeing much with it in the sent and figure of the flowers, but different much in the greene leaves. It is very sweet, very various, very hardy, easily encreast, and soone at perfection, of fine forme, and beautiful colours, and agrees admirably well with ye Climate, soe it may seeme for all these good qualityes not inferiour to any flower this Countrey can produce'.

He indicates that Bear's Ears come in many colours, using words for the hues which have disappeared from our vocabularies but which are more detailed and accurate than the ones we use – and infinitely more poetic. Eleanour Sinclair Rhode in her introduction to *The Garden Book,* provided a list of these colour words.

Sir Thomas's colour-comparisons are equally charming: deare colour, dove colour, mouse

SIR THOMAS'S COLOURS

Amaranthe	purple
Aurora	deep orange
Bertino	blue-grey
Celadon	pale green
Furille mort or feuille mort	dead leaf colour
Gilvus	very pale red
Gridelin or grizeli, from *gris du lin*	the grey of flax
Isabella	greyish yellow
Minimme	dun colour, from colour of the Minim Friar's robe
Murrey	mulberry
Quoist	colour of a dove's breast (stockdoves were called Quees or Quiese)
Watchet	sky blue
Philomot	also colour of a dead leaf
Ortment	bright yellow
Verdigreese	rusty green
Indico	indigo blue
Stamell	a red, inferior in brilliancy to scarlet

colour, sand colour, willow colour – and what could be more enchanting than 'needlework pale peach'?

While describes his Bear's Ears mainly by colour, he is aware that some have names 'imposed' upon them. Within these he lumps together the raiser's name (a familiar one, Tuggeys, for example) with what Rea will call 'fantastical' names such as 'Belle Brunette'. (Could this be the same *Brunette* praised in Franeau's 1616 *Jardin d'Hyver*?)

Sir Thomas finished the manuscript in 1659, the same year in which Oliver Cromwell's son Richard fell from power. It was written with a beautiful, regular hand in a thick quarto book bound in brown calf, but some pages must have remained blank for he continued to add further notes over the next few years. Amongst them are, 'bear's ears grown in 1661'. First was his 'largest best', which included several Leathercoats, 'Yeoman of Kent', a Dearecolor and a Dovecolor; secondly his 'middle sized', which included several yellows, 'Blacke Emperor, rose's olive, a good deepe olive sadder than Yeoman of Kent'; and lastly his three 'least flowered', a red, 'Prince of Orange' and 'Crimson Velvet'.

His last entry dates from 1670 and is a list of auriculas purchased from George Ricketts of Hoxton, who was described by Rea as 'often remembered as the best and most faithful Florist now about London'. A single cost Sir Thomas a shilling and a Double, 4 shillings the root. The equivalent prices today (according to the National Archive Converter, which I use throughout for this purpose) being ± £4.00 and £16.00 respectively.

It is of interest that by 1670 Sir Thomas is using the word 'Auriculars' rather than Bear's Ears (as the spelling was not standardized, one sometimes finds an 'r' at the end) and also that he comments that one plant died and another proved to be 'the wrong sort', indicating how little nurseries have changed.

Sir Thomas Hanmer became the local MP and lived the rest of his life at Bettisfield surrounded by his garden and his family. On the first page of the manuscript is a tiny scribbled note to the effect that, 'My grandchild Thomas Hanmer was born at Bettisfield on Monday betwixt ten and eleven at night being the twenty-fourth of September 1677'. The child, another Sir Thomas Hanmer, grew up to become Speaker to the House of Commons, and the date proves that Hanmer was still adding notes to his *Garden Book* some twenty years after its ostensible completion. That it was intended for publication is apparent from the fact that it is addressed at times to 'the reader' and sad though it is that it lay forgotten for almost three centuries, its eventual publication presented us with one of the greatest treasures of garden literature.

SAMUEL GILBERT'S *FLORIST'S VADE-MECUM*

Another small treasure of the same ilk as the *Garden Book* is Samuel Gilbert's *Florist's Vade-Mecum*

published in 1682. Gilbert (d. 1692), rector of Quatt and chaplain to Lady Gerard of Bromley, was married to John Rea's daughter Minerva. They all lived together at Kinlet, and when Rea died his nursery passed to the couple.

Gilbert stamps his personality on his book from the beginning, telling the reader that the 'least lover of flowers is welcome to enter' (his book) but not 'those who think it a Divertisement or too easie or effeminate, preferring a piece of Bacon or Cabbage before nature's choicest dishes'.

He acknowledges that he has gained from 'being inform'd by my long converse with the best florist of his time, Mr John Rea, my father in law whose skill and collection were alike famous', but he is keen to assert his own authority saying, 'since his death most of each in my possession newer flowers and their wayes of management and production I have attained'. He also declares that he intends to 'leave out many obsolete and over dated flowers to make room for many new ones' and also 'all or any Bumbastick words that our last author in Octavo (surely a reflection on Rea) declaims against, yet uses'.

Florists' flowers were becoming extremely popular, and Gilbert is critical of greedy nurserymen and their practices. His book, he says, is 'published to … the disadvantage of the Mercenary Flower Catchers about London or some that are of the same stamp scattered up and down the Countrey, Fathering new names on Old Flowers to enhance their price'. London is probably mentioned because nurseries were proliferating there; by 1690 some fifteen nurseries were trading.

He also indicates that florists are becoming more discerning and famously describes some flowers as 'trifles adored amongst country women in their gardens but of no esteem to a Florist who is taken up with things of more value'.

Gilbert is aware that the increase in popularity has resulted in high prices. He mentions those 'from one, two, three, four, and five pounds a root' and adds 'to close with the best last, two rare striped Auriculas their price bespeaks them,

Facing page: Lord Saye en Sele.

Prince John.

the one at four and the other nearer five pounds,' and he then makes the much-quoted claim of outrageous pricing: 'I have been sold [does he mean told?] for twenty as I have been informed they may now be cheaper, and are in the hands of Peter Egerton of Boughton near Chester Esq. viz The double strip'd & White. The double very large and full of leaves purple and yellow the two choicest rarities of Flora's Cabinet'. A pound sterling in 1680 was the equivalent of ± £80.00 today. Thus when Gilbert speaks of the plant which sold for twenty pounds one can only wonder at the payment of the equivalent of £1670.00 for such a plant. The annual wage a head gardener in Cheshire received in 1683 was £60.00 (about the same as a clergyman), so the cost of this auricula would have represented a third of his annual income. But was Gilbert reliable? We shall see.

Regarding Bear's Ears, Gilbert divides them into Single, Self colour, Single striped, Double Self colour and Double striped flower. This is the first time that we have seen an auricula classified as a 'Self'.

Gilbert's list follows Rea's with a few additions. Yellows have to be multi-trussed and deeply coloured otherwise 'not worth a farthing'. Leathercoats are still esteemed and come in tones of Liver colour with gray eye, Hair colour, Clove colour, Willow Colour, Mouse colour, Cinnamon,

Greenish hair colour, Light Tawney & White. The new fashionable auricula is 'Blazing Star' 'of a very deep murrish liver colour with a snowy white eye as big as the whole of another Flower'. Of the reds he mentions Mrs Austin's. He also says: 'There are some of Mr Jacob Roberts raising that are good flowers, who keeps the Physick Garden in Oxford.' (This solves a small mystery. I could never understand why Sacheverell Sitwell referred to Mr *Roberts* as being Keeper of the Oxford Botanic Garden, when the Bobarts were well known to have held this position. I realize now that he got his information from Gilbert, thus casting doubts on his, Gilbert's, reliability.)

Doubles have also developed and are much admired, but it is certain that Stripes were the 'enobled' auriculas of the day, and some of the combinations sound amazing: 'dull flesh colour and lemmon, liver colour and yellow broad stripes, blond colour streaked with yellow, dark and gold, fine violet and white, buffe and lemon, hair colour and lemon, philomot and leather colour, dark hair colour streaked with lighter, needlework pale peach and white in small streaks'.

Gilbert ends with a poem which once again has echoes of Franeau's elegy in *Le Jardin d'Hyver*:

See how the Beares Eares in their several dresses
(That yet no Poet's pen expresses.)
Each head adorned with such rich attire
Which Fools and Clowns may slight, which skilled
    admire
Their gold, their purples, scarlets, crimson dies
Their darker and lighter hair'd diversities
With all their pretty shades and Ornaments
Their parti-colour'd coats and pleasing scents
Gold laid on scarlet, silver on the blew
With sparkling eyes to take the eyes of you
Mixt colours, many more to please that sense
Other with rich and great magnificence
In double Ruffs, with gold and silver laced
On purple crimson and so neatly placed
Ransack Flora's wardrobe, none sure can bring
More taking Ornaments t'adorn the Spring.

Facing page: Rajah.

ALEXANDER MARSHALL'S *FLORILEGIUM*

The written records of Bobart, Rea, Hanmer and Gilbert give us elaborate descriptions of auriculas, and we can examine the dried specimens of Bobart's *Hortus Siccus* for further clues. However the advent of the florilegium, here as on the continent, is about to provide us with much clearer evidence of ways in which florists' flowers were changing. Used by plant collectors and the owners of great gardens to record their precious plants both for their own enjoyment and in order to show off to other enthusiasts, most were composed of etchings and engravings. Very occasionally a unique hand-painted example was made. Alexander Marshall's *Florilegium* is a rare British survivor of this genre.

Little is known about Marshall. He was thought to have been born around 1620, possibly in France. His friend the polymath and educationalist, Samuel Hartlib (c.1600–1662) mentions in his diary that Marshall was 'A Merchant' who had 'lived some years in Fraunce, speaking French perfectly' and that he was 'one of the greatest florists and dealers for all manner of Roots, Plantes and seeds from the Indies and elsewhere'. The foreword written in 1760 by Dr William Friend who inherited the original manuscript, however, claims it as the 'Work of a Gentleman' who had 'an independent fortune and painted merely for his own Amusement'. Marshall, in common which many other 'curious gentlemen' also had a remarkable cabinet of curiosities and according to Hartlib was 'stupendiously excellent in all manner of Insects.' These he often includes in his paintings, adding to their charm.

In 1641 he was living in south Lambeth with John Tradescant the Younger. It is thought that he painted a florilegium of Tradescant's garden, as there is an entry in the inventory of the Ark describing a volume as containing 'Mr Tradescant's choicest Flowers and Plants, exquisitely limned in vellum by Mr Alex: Marshall.' Unfortunately this has been lost. Thirty-three of Marshall's botanical paintings dating from this period are, however, to be found in the British Museum. It is also now thought that Marshall could have painted the picture of John Tradescant the Elder which is in the Ashmolean Museum in Oxford, which was previously attributed to Cornelius de Neve. In 1650 Marshall moved to Ham in Surrey, and in 1653 he was living in Islington where he had a garden 'on John Dawes land'.

Bishop Compton

In 1667 Marshall moved to Winchester to take the post of Steward to Henry Compton, brother of the 3rd Earl of Northampton. Henry Compton subsequently became Bishop of Oxford and later in 1675, Bishop of London, at which stage he moved into Fulham Palace. Charles I had appointed Bishop Compton as tutor to the Princesses Mary and Anne, daughters of the Duke of York, in order that they should receive Protestant instruction. After the death of Charles I, James II had Bishop Compton suspended, but Mary and Anne, both destined to be Queens of England, remained close to him and Mary assisted in his rehabilitation. He in turn supported the claim of Mary and her husband William of Orange to the British throne.

At Fulham Palace the Bishop developed his thirty-acre garden with the assistance of his gardener George London (born c.1640). London went on to become a very well known and very rich nurseryman, earning large sums from this work as well as the profits from the nursery. His partner Henry Wise, who had been apprenticed to John Rose, did even better – as gardener to Queen Anne and George I, he received £1,600 per annum – equivalent to ±£120,500 today, an astronomical sum at the time. The bishop was an avid plant collector and is credited with importing some forty new species from America and growing the first coffee tree in England in his heated stove house. John Evelyn visited the gardens in 1681 and pronounced them remarkable.

When the Bishop took up his London appointment Marshall moved with him to Fulham Palace. It was here in the Bishop's garden of a thousand plants that Marshall undoubtedly found a good number of the subjects for his florilegium. He depicts a wide variety of flowers: roses and exotics

Facing page: Lovebird.

but also simple wild flowers. He includes fashion-able florists' flowers; carnations, anemones, tulips – and thirty-eight auriculas. Not all his flowers are 'perfect' specimens; blemishes on leaves and holes made by his beloved insects add realism as do the drips of water on some plants.

Marshall's auriculas give us the first vivid colour images of English-grown auriculas. They also indi-cate that Doubles in fact had been in existence some years before Rea's book was published.

Stripes were by now amongst the most fashion-able auriculas. Florists had worked to 'improve' them until they reached the quality depicted by Marshall and, somewhat later, Furber. Over half of the flowers depicted by Marshall show a degree of striping. There is a delectable mauve striped with deep yellow, and a rare yellow double striped with white.

By pure chance striping chimed with the aes-thetic of the period. It could however have been quite different. The anonymous Florist of Bath, writing of the 'flakes' or stripes in 1732, relates that 'some authors that have treated of flowers have attributed these stripes to the want of sap, and others to the weakness of or sickness of the plant'. How easily they could have simply been cast aside.

In Marshall's images the trusses show and average of six pips, some in bud. Some, but not all, show a defined eye with a circle of meal. The petals are very varied in form, some being rounded, others more pointed. One flower appears to be a hose-in-hose mutation. The leaves, some smooth, some notched, appear in some cases to be some-what 'primrosey', and most show a little farina. These plants might not impress a modern judge,

but they do afford us insights into the look of the auriculas of this period.

Brigitte Wachsmuth made the interesting point that in these images, as Marshall always represents the plants with one pip directly face-on to the viewer and showing a regular eye, we are begin-ning to see the idealization of the auricula which was to take over nineteenth century paintings. This she sees as indicating that 'standards of perfection had emerged already, at least on a seminal stage'. Further it is worth noting that nearly all the pips are thum-eyed, indicating that even at this date this was *de rigueur*.

Various other factors enabled a more accurate scientific approach to illustration, one of which was the increased availability of the microscope. This had been invented in 1590 by the Dutchman Zacharias Janssen and his son, and in 1665 Robert Hooke published *Micrographia* which effectively revealed completely new aspects of the natural world. Nehemiah Grew (1641–1712) Secretary of the Royal Society spent twenty years compiling his *Anatomy of Plants* which was published in 1682. Grew studied the interior 'elegancies' of flowers, which were normally unseen by the human eye, and wondered as to their functions. Regarding the stamens of flowers which he called their 'attire' he gradually came to the conclusion that 'the attire doth serve, as the male, for the generation of the seed', thus effectively launching the concept of plant sexuality fifty years before Linnaeus. He also investigated 'that fine white flour or powder, which lies over the leaves of some plants of the Bears' Ear', wondering what its purpose was – a question explored by Biffen from the 1920s to the 1940s but not yet fully answered even now.

Facing page: Blue Velvet.

CHAPTER SIX

Continental Developments

On the continent the financial bubble of Tulipomania burst in 1637, resulting in the prohibition of buying and selling tulips and a general fall in the prices of flowers. Although some people suffered commercially, however, the passion for florists' flowers continued unabated into the eighteenth century.

FLORISTS' FLOWERS IN LEIDEN

The continued buoyancy of the floral market is confirmed by the publication of a book in 1703 *The Dutch Gardener* by Hendrik van Oosten of Leiden. Although much of it was plagiarized from Monstereul's fifty-year-old *Le Floriste François*, it leaves one in no doubt that florists' flowers were still highly regarded. If, claims the author, the 'young Lovers of Flowers' at whom this book is aimed 'follow the path that is here chalked they will speedily get into the High road that leads to a Garden ... which will prove to be an agreeable seat of Happiness'.

Van Oosten, for whom the tulip was always The Queen of Flowers, gives precise growing instructions – 'seeds should be sown in a north wind under a waning moon'. He has no patience with 'false florists who, like swine love to scuffle through our Flower Gardens, to carry off their Riches by their Greatness and Impudence'. He further says that one must distinguish between the 'true Sons of Flora' and mere dealers who 'promote the growth of flowers as long as they can put the commodity to good advantage'.

Van Oosten also gives us an interesting picture of the equivalents of the florist feasts in the Low countries – although apparently they were more frugal than those in Britain. 'When the Publick buying and selling of Tulips was prohibited, the florists fell to trucking and private selling; but because this could not be done without Animositie, thereupon the *Flemish* Florists elected a Fraternity in the Cities; and took St Dorothea to be their Patroness, and the Syndicus to be Judge of the Differences that may arise by their Trucking.' He differentiates between the Flemish and the Dutch: 'The *Dutch* keep in this Matter another Rule; they meet together on a certain Day, when Tulips are in their full Bloom, and choose, after having seen the chief Gardens of the Florists, and taken a friendly and frugal Dinner together, one of the Company to Judge the Differences.'

We can get some idea of the Dutch auriculas of the period from two more herbaria at Leiden. Nicholaas Meerburg (1733–1814) head gardener of the Leiden Botanic Garden, included two auriculas in his herbarium, probably collected from the Leiden gardens. Another collection featuring twelve *Auricula ursi* is that of Adriaan van Royen (1704–99) and his nephew David van Royen (1727–99) who were also both directors of this garden. I have not seen these specimens myself, but from pictures published in the NAPS Northern Yearbook 1998, I gather that some paste remains, that some are striped, there is a yellow and a blue and one with a slot shaped tube shows slight shading. They are all labelled simply *Auricula ursi*.

While herbarium specimens suffer from the passing of time, paintings however, can remain pristine. One such featuring florists' flowers is *Month of April* by Peeter Snijers painted in 1727. This lovely painting shows a young woman in the foreground of an ornate garden, dressed in loose gardening clothes and talking to her servant who holds a basket of vegetables. There are tulips and other florists' flowers in containers at the front of the picture, but the woman is holding a bunch of red auriculas in her hand, and a terracotta pot containing a reddish striped one is on a stand beside her and two more of the same type are in pots in the foreground.

FRANCE
Charles Guénin's *Traité*

The first book devoted entirely to the auricula appeared in France in 1732. The *Traité de la culture parfaite de l'oreille d'ours ou auricule* is by 'Un Curieux de Province' who signed himself, 'Un Ingénu'. The author is thought to have been a Charles Guénin (Ingénu' is an anagram of his surname), a passionate florist by inclination and a tax collector by occupation. It is believed that he adopted the pseudonym because he had no official permission to print a book.

There were in fact, three editions: one in 1732; a second in 1735 (in which the title was slightly different and which contained much additional material) and in 1738, the much shorter '*Nouveau traité*' devoted only to cultivation. Each edition varied in content and size, being 133, 237 and 74 pages respectively. The first two were said to have been published in Brussels and the third in Paris. The Brussels claim however is inaccurate, as the printer mentioned had died two years before the first edition and both print and paper are Parisian. These books are extremely rare; only five copies are known to exist.

Some copies of the second edition bore what must in fact be the first illustration of an auricula theatre – that is, an arrangement of shelving for their display – to have been depicted. In it an odd individual in a nightcap points to an auricula theatre overrun with mice above which hangs a scroll bearing the words, '*Quisque suos*' [Each to his Own]. The caption below this image is, '*Chacun Aime, Entretient Les Siens. L'Auricules Nourit Les Miens*' [Everyone takes care of his own (obsession). The auricula nourishes mine]. Perhaps the thing most people remember about the *Nouveau*

Traité is the frontispiece showing an illustration of the auricula theatre or *buffet* decorated with fools' caps and bearing the caption '*Chacun à sa Marotte*'. In this rather enigmatic caption *marotte* refers to a craze which could lead to folly; the fools' caps echo the images which were circulated in Holland at the time of tulipomania.

The second edition contains the most information. Some items are in prose, others in verse by a M. Picart. The introduction suggests that this edition has been produced because insufficient copies of the first were published and some of the *curieux* were disappointed.

Guénin proclaims that the *oreille d'ours*, or Bear's Ear, is the equal of the tulip, with the advantages of being green all year, having a sweet scent, making *beaux bouquets* (especially the *pures* and the *bizarres*) and flowering twice a year. An interest in plants, he declares, is an innocent pursuit but not if it leads to outrageous or imprudent expenditure, when it is '*folie alors*'.

He describes three types: *Pures* or colours, which we would call Selfs; *Panachées* or *Tracées*, Stripes of two colours; and the *Bizarres*, Stripes of several colours.

He refers to the foliage, pointing out – and this is an important fact seldom stated – that the differences in the leaves help the florist to recognize the flower, especially when someone has removed the label ... The stem, he says, must be strong and hold the truss when all pips are open but a little wire hook painted green can, if the flower is exceptional and it is tastefully done, be placed 'so as to embrace the stem'. The pips should be round and flat and should not form a 'little windmill'. The petals should be ample, thick, velvety, satiny, glossy or transparent. Proportion is essential: '*Il faut de la proportion en tout*'.

In *Pures* and *Panachées* it does not seem that paste on the circle was admired, as he advises that letting them flower in sun and rain helps to remove it – and adds that some florists take it off with a damp paintbrush. The stamens 'usually seven in number make a little yellow feature in the eye'. He also mentions green stamens 'like wood moss' which fill the eye but do not look as good. The flower should be thrum eyed (that is, with stamens and anthers visible at the top of the tube);

White Wings.

if instead there is only one pistil, *javelot* or *dard,* the plant is absolutely to be thrown out.

Panachées he does not consider of the first rank but finds acceptable if glossy and velvety with stripes that are clear and well coloured from base to tip. The circle must be round, if hexagonal it is unacceptable. There are two types of *Bizarres;* old and new. The old have a circle of gold or white. The new are brought from England or raised from their seed and 'show an admirable variety of colours, some quite opposite like white and black, completely covered with white powder which being doubled on the circle make them very bright and distinguished'. He adds that the well-rounded ones are highly esteemed and very rare, and it is good if you raise one from 500 seeds.

Pures are apparently preferred to *Panachées* and *Bizarres* because they are bigger and more velvety. Some are darkened around the circle, these are called *Transparents, Lactées* and *Nuancés*. Some of these have such a clear, dark ring that they almost seem a fourth sort, different from the other *Pures*.

The finest flowers in the world, however, are the fine dark velvety shaded *Pures*, the *Ombrées*, where the brown or black colour shades from the middle of the petal towards the edge. Examples are *Le Feu Ombrée, Le Feu Tigresse, Le Panebroek, Le Panerock* and *La Reine Elizabeth*. Even so, *le Fleuriste n'est jamais content* [the florist is never content] he always wants more and bigger.

He gives the names of some of the enthusiasts who permit visits to their collections between 20 April and 10 May and lists towns and villages of Northern France and the Low Countries where they can be found. He observes that it is good to see that is often the workers who raise the most beautiful plants *'la nature n'ayant aucun regard particulier pour les dignitiez'* [nature not paying much attention to dignitaries]. His list encompasses a good cross-section of society, including nobles, magistrates, a royal secretary, a valet of the Queen, army officers, canons, priests, monks, lawyers, doctors, apothecaries, a music teacher, merchants, a carpenter, a joiner – and even a couple of women: Mademoiselle de la Motte, niece of M. Desmay and Madame la Clerc la Jeune.

Theatrical Display

Tournai, where Clusius' correspondent M. Plateau had cultivated auriculas in the 1580s and where one of Franeau's *curieux* lived in 1616, was still an auricula stronghold and must surely have offered the most fascinating visit of all. For here the Abbot, prior and monks of the Abbey of St Michael apparently had at least fifteen theatres on view and received visitors 'with a politeness and affability of manner which is easier to imagine than describe'. Guénin makes a comment, as true now as then, that the sight of a quantity of bear's ears flowering together will charm anyone, not just connoisseurs. He describes the theatre or buffet used to display the bear's ears as being made of planks with a roof high enough to allow air to circulate, painted black so that the flowers stand out.

The notion of displaying flowers in this way was not entirely new, as in discussing display, Valnay in 1696 had written that a 'Theatre of Flowers' could be composed of tulips, anemones, carnations or bear's ears. He went on to describe one which a tulip fancier had showed him, 'In the middle of the room, on a very large table, he made a theatre of five or six long tiers of 4 to 6 *pouces* & raised one over the other at the same height, he covered them with a green carpet and cut the tulips so perfectly so that he put each one in a small flask ... (and) arranged the flasks on the tiers.'

Facing page: Joy.

Francois-Xavier Mallet in *La Beauté de Nature* of 1775 described making a summer stage in the form of a pyramid in which flowers could be combined so that they lasted for months. 'The auricula is the first flower to be entered into the theatre among those of premier order; following the ranunculus in the pyramid & then the carnation completes it'.

J.P. Moet mentions displaying the plants on staging in his 1754 *Traite de la culture des renocelle, des oeillets, des aurcules et des tulips*, making the same point about a quantity of pots of Bear's Ears attracting everyone. Much of what Moet wrote echoes Guénin. He too is dismissive of the wrong type of florist, especially the one 'with a heart of stone who would rather crush and destroy the spare offsets of their most beautiful plants rather than enrich a friend'. He discusses the same three types as Guénin. *Pures* are still the preferred type and within *Pures*, the *Transparentes* are the most esteemed. He also comments that although *Panachées* are no longer of the first rank, some people still like them, but their '*panaches*' must be clean and well defined, which is rare.

He lists some *Bizarres* of supposedly English provenance although the names scarcely reflect this: 'L'Afriquain' bred from 'Merveille du Monde', a velvety, almost black purple with a green edge; 'Cryrus' striped dark crimson, very velvety edged green; 'Persée' striped purple and black with traces of velvety pale purple and a chamois eye; 'Passe-dominant', coffee colour with traces of sea green; 'Le Brilliant' a velvety light coffee colour, striped yellow; and 'Bizarre Supreme', violet purple and white with tracings of bright and brilliant sea green which was also bred from 'Merveille du Monde'.

GERMAN FLORILEGIA
Volkamer's Engravings

In Germany too, there are plenty of Stripes, Doubles and distinctive colours described in *Flora Noribergensis, The Nurnbergishen Hesperides* which Johann Christoph Volkamer (1644–1720) published in two volumes between 1708 and 1714. Although these engravings are mainly of citrus fruit (orangeries were the height of fashion) there are sixty-six auriculas illustrated. The unusual

thing about these images is that the fruit or flowers are depicted floating in the sky beneath which are wonderfully ornate landscapes of Italianate palazzi and formal gardens and even some naval scenes.

Volkamer cultivated a garden in the Gostenhof district of Nuremberg, and it is thought that the auriculas come from his garden or that of his brother. They appear attractively set against a skyscape, with a background of the village of Grundlach and what looks like an estate, captioned *Im Bretzen Garten* below.

The auriculas are depicted in three plates in the first volume. In most cases single pips are shown and there are two Doubles and a number of Stripes. The forms are very varied. In the original volumes the images were uncoloured, but hand-coloured versions were later produced. As always some allowance must be made for the fact that the colourists were not seeing the live plant – but what is unusual in this work is that the text contains a detailed description of each auricula. These were published in the NAPS Southern Yearbook 1993, translated by Ken Saint.

We read of leaf forms and wonderful petal colours: ferruginous striped with sulphur, pale leather, orange flaming into red, stripes of brown, purple, red and gold-yellow, purple coloured with tongues of sulphur and pale red spotted double flowers. These descriptions, coupled with the illustrations, offer us a particularly full picture of the auriculas growing in Germany early in the eighteenth century. Of the sixty-six only five bear cultivar names, all Dutch: 'Hollandse Leeuw', 'Bifard Aleppe', 'Der Groote Draak', 'Von Tage' and 'Bruydegam'.

Simula's Paintings

Another interesting German florilegium, *Flora Exotica*, was painted by Johann Gottgried Simula for the Imperial Count Johann Georg Dernath in the 1720s. The Count was a keen gardener, and the plants depicted are from his garden at Sierhagen (Syrhagen) in Schleswig Holstein. The park and garden were very important to the Count

Facing page: Teem.

and indeed to his whole family; his children would go out with their pony wagon and spread sand onto the garden paths. In 1717 the Count was sending pineapple and Indian plants to a friend in Würzburg, and in 1726 Italian gardeners were expected. The diary of the Count's secretary also mentions putting out the auriculas – 409 pots of them. The aim of the florilegium as usual was to preserve the plants for posterity and also to show the Count's success in plant breeding. Many of the plants depicted in the florilegium bear the initial 'S' to indicate they were raised by him at Syrhagen.

The paintings show a good range of colours, with leaves in silvery greys and varying shades of green. The auriculas are named, the names being contained in attractive decorative swags which help to convey period atmosphere. There are some forty depicted, the majority being German with the home-bred auriculas bearing the 'S'. Some are Dutch, 'Hollandishe Leuw', 'Geeronde Standart' and some English, 'William Triumphante'. About a third are Painted Ladies – there rendered phonetically by the artist as *Paindit Laedis*. This was a term used in the Dutch trade to delineate the varieties with farina, and although it often implies that they were imported from England, here we see P.L. 'Leuw' and P.L. 'Suiver Keit' both bearing Dutch names. The majority appear to be stripes, but of these only some are specifically labelled BYS, meaning *Bisarden* or striped. There are some handsome dark Selfs.

We can see some development in auricula types here. Several have very pointed petals, and there is a green tipped auricula next to the Painted Lady 'Souverain S' which shows possible virescence (to be discussed shortly). Another, 'Theseus', shows a brownish colour which shades into buff in the way of an Alpine. Unfortunately the Count probably spent more money on his garden than he could afford, for in 1730, only four years after those Italian gardeners were so eagerly anticipated, the florilegium was sold at the Dernath bankruptcy sale, from whence it came via intermediate owners to the Library of the Natural History Museum in London.

Weinmann's Mezzotints

Yet another German work which depicts auriculas is Johann Weinmann's four-volume *Phytanthoza Iconographia* containing some 9,000 plant images. Weinmann (1683–1741) was an apothecary from Regensburg and this, his life's work, was one of the first botanical books to contain the new colour-printed mezzotints, a development in printing that could be somewhat smudgy; aquatints were found to be more suitable for scientific subjects. It could also be counted amongst the last of the herbals.

The work was published from 1735 in half-yearly instalments and sadly Weinmann died before the work was finished. Linnaeus was amongst those who had a hand in its completion. The painter Georg Dionysius Ehret (1708–1770) depicted some of the flowers in these works before coming to England, and as the auriculas appear early in the first volume he may in fact have been responsible for them.

There are seventy-four auricula illustrations of eighteen varieties and five plates of single pips. The auriculas, captioned only as *Auricula ursi* followed by a description, show great diversity. Some here also have the very pointed petals (captioned *flore stellato*) and several have quite pronounced green tips (one with a magenta body colour is captioned *flore magno ex rubro et viridi mixto*) – a further confirmation that virescence was developing in Europe at this period. This is of interest because whereas the advent of the Green Edge was hailed in England as a marvel and thereafter Edges reigned supreme, in Europe it was far less esteemed. The Alpine type of shaded auricula which was also developing was about to take centre stage. So clear was the distinction that Edges became known as 'English' Auriculas, and the Alpine type, 'Liegois' or 'Luiker' Auriculas. David Tarver made the astute comment in an article that the severity of form of the Edge made it 'the ideal subject for a nation of competitive puritans'.

The Flower Books of Karlsruhe

Of course people continued to collect all types, and plenty of Stripes and Doubles are to be found in the amazing *Flower Books of Karlsruhe*, which were painted for Karl Wilhelm III, Margrave of Baden Durlach (1679–1738), a true gardening prince. The French had plundered his kingdom in 1689 and he attempted a programme of rebuilding, moving his whole court from Durlach and in 1715 founding the town of Karlsruhe (Karl's Peace) in the nearby forest. The baroque city was designed to fan out around his *Residenz*, and within a few decades he had established a magnificent garden.

Karl Wilhelm was a hands-on gardener. He had studied botany in Holland, but he liked nothing better than to don gardener's clothes and dig his own borders. Above all he was a great plant collector who amassed some 5,000 tulips, 600 carnations and 500 auriculas from all over Europe. He left handwritten plant inventories from the years 1723–36 with listings of what had been bought for each year. In 1727 for example there are six listings of 212 different auriculas.

Karl Wilhelm's private life was the subject of considerable gossip, as he had a 'harem' of sixty young 'Tulip Girls' from the local villages. They were expected to sing and dance for him, serve him at table and ride out with him wearing hussar's uniforms. There was also a building on the estate, decorated in oriental style with sofas and cushions, where food was served and other 'amusements' took place … In return, the Tulip Girls were apparently given an exceptionally good education in all aspects of arts and sciences.

Karl Wilhelm also commissioned a series of paintings depicting the choice blooms of his collection, but sadly many of these were lost in the bombings of the Second World War. By the good fortune of their being elsewhere, a few did survive. On Plate 70 of the *Karlsruhen Tulpenbuch* at the Badishe Ladesbibliotek, twenty-four pips are depicted.

According to Brigitte Wachsmuth (to whom I am indebted for this information), an even more interesting series is found at Baden Wurttemberg's public record office. It consists of a portfolio of 159 single postcard sheets, each one depicting a different auricula pip. They cover the whole range: Doubles, Stripes, early Edges, together with Selfs and shaded prototypes of Luiker or Alpine types and some PLs or Painted Ladies. From the names one can deduce that most are Dutch, but there is also a 'Stra berrie' (Strawberry) and a 'Prinz Wallis' (Prince of Wales), which indicate an English origin. Some of the paintings are signed by court painters, and attached to others are hand written comments such as 'right' 'not quite right' and 'too violet brown', implying that someone, maybe a tutor, was comparing the painting with the real plant. Each one is signed and some names are in the feminine form, so could painting these auricula paintings have formed part of the education of the Tulip girls? Fittingly, Karl Wilhelm died, hoe in hand, while working on his tulip beds.

Trew's *Hortus Nitidissimus*

Karl Wilhelm's head gardener Christian Thran grew and sold auriculas, some of which were bought by Christoph Jacob Trew (1695–1769) who was responsible for another important work, the *Hortus Nitidissimus*. Trew was a doctor who keenly promoted the sciences, especially botany. He was also an amateur gardener who corresponded with many of the great scientists and horticulturalists of the period and accumulated a collection of letters by past savants which is invaluable to historians today.

The *Hortus Nitidissimus* was composed of engraved plates, many by Georg Dionysus Ehret, accompanied by notes on cultivation. It was published as a part-work between the years 1750 and 1785, and the fact that many sections got lost or separated over the years accounts for its rarity as a whole. In England one copy is found in Kew and another in the Natural History Museum, and both of these have been digitalized and combined to form an Ideal Copy combining all plates and articles.

There are two auricula plates. One by Ehret (Plate 13) depicts the auricula 'Danae', a white with yellow centre and red with deep reddish mauve striped edge. The other auricula (Plate 39) is by an unknown artist and shows the 'Herzon von Cumberland' (Duke of Cumberland), a purple with five pips.

The text relating to auriculas begins with what appears to be an odd claim about the origin of the plant. 'Travelling business men, passing through, once came in France to a meadow with faded auriculas. The shine and scent of these wild

Rosebud.

they are changeable and often assume the colour of the stripes all over'. Luikish auriculas, on the other hand 'have only one colour. One subdivides them into single colour and mirrored ones. The mirrored ones are those that carry at the base of their petals a mirror of a different colour resembling a peacock feather'.

Doubles, at one time double the price, are disposed of rather disparagingly as flowers which 'occur both among the English and the Luikish ones but they stand in low esteem'.

A further point of interest is that standards are beginning to be formulated.

TREW'S STANDARDS OF BEAUTY

The beauty of an auricular, be it English or Luiker, depends on the following:

1) that the flower be large and that there should be many flowers,
2) that it should have a free-standing and tall peduncle,
3) the flower must be of beautiful colour and marking,
4) the flower must be well rounded and the tepals turned slightly outwards,
5) the flower must not have a stigma (button) but an eye,
6) if it is an English auricula, the stripes have to be pure and distinct.

---

flowers appeared to them to be so lovely, that they took various sods and brought them to Flanders. From there the flower returned to its homeland and was as an entirely new plant, received and admired'. If however, one substitutes 'Windish-Matrei' for France and 'peasants' for travelling businessmen and takes into account the number of times the tale must have been told down the generations, isn't there perhaps an echo of the von Wulfen story?

A definition of the two types is offered. 'The English Auriculas are the striped and the powdered ones, or as they are now called, the laquered ones. They are divided, in turn into *picottes, picottebizards*, and *bizards*. The *picottes* are those with dots and very fine stripes and only two colours, the *picottebizards* are more colourful and they are also delicately striped. The *bizards* have broad stripes;

Regarding English taste, we also learn that 'according to the present taste of most flower enthusiasts the English value the green striped one and those which have the *feuille-mort* colour, the sky blue and violet ones most. This depends however on the discretion of every individual. It suffices to be beautiful, for the flowers to have the above named six characteristics. Even if some prefer the English to the Luikish ones, no distinct message can be gained from this'.

Facing page: Sirius.

Regarding names he states, 'Every flower enthusiast has the right to name those flowers that he grows from seeds just as a father names his children.' This sounds eminently sensible until we read that, 'it retains this name until someone else decides to rename it'. A couple of auriculas are named: 'Arcus Triumphalis' 'by no means among those of the first order' and 'Gloria Mundi' which 'surpasses the former by much'.

The notes for cultivation, which cover sowing seed, taking offsets and general care, are fascinating and sometimes amusing. On sowing seed, 'One need not consider any full moon or celestial calendar signs because one sows the seed in soil and not on the moon,' or 'Count Crequi Frohans in Picardie has invented a dibble with a handle making it easier for the worker to lift the soil ... In Germany such Counts are rare'.

One of the most important works of this fruitful period of German floricultural literature was *Der Blumist*, a four-volume work by Johann Nicolaus Weissmantel published in 1783, of which Volume 2 deals with the auricula. It contains no less than 387 pages specifically treating the auricula, together with a register and lists of types. As this created a demand for the plants Weissmantel soon added a catalogue with hand-painted illustrations and a price list. Weissmantel was not content with the division of auriculas into Luiker and English types and tried to add a third category which he called 'Mulattos', but they did not gain recognition.

In 1791 J. Neuenhahn produced a book *Uber dier Auriklesysteme,* which purported to be an entirely new classification of auriculas. It would appear that the criteria for the beauty of the auricula was similar to that in England but not quite so strictly delineated. As a wider range of forms was acceptable it did mean a greater gene pool was available.

From around 1780 auriculas inspired designers in Germany, finding their way onto some of the exquisite Meissen, Thuringian and Loosdrecter porcelain.

The poet Goethe (1749–1832) made a comment about auriculas in his 1809 novel, *Elective Affinities*. In this strange work in which the human characters are brought together as if in a chemical experiment; a garden is being planned, and the old gardener who had in the past perfectly understood what to do including 'growing cuttings from the carnations and auriculas' is baffled by 'the new ornamental shrubs and fashionable flowers.' The implication here is that the auricula has fallen out of fashion.

Goethe himself however, was an auricula lover and is reported to have visited his friend Duke Carl August at Belvedere Castle, where he was shown a collection of some 400. Apparently he only remarked on the difference between the Luiker and English types, which was ironic as had he noticed any green-edged specimens it would have confirmed the famous remark he made in his *Italian Journey* of 1787 that 'Anyway you look at it, the plant is only leaf'. Carl August's court gardener Johann Friedrich Reichart published a catalogue *Hortus Reichartienis*, offering 400 varieties from Holland and England for sale. Here too, incredible prices were paid.

Auriculas remained popular on the continent throughout the eighteenth century. Holland, still one of the chief suppliers, had however, been involved in three wars with England. Religious strife continued, Catholics were penalized in England, and in 1685 Louis XIV revoked the edict of Nantes and another wave of Huguenots fled seeking refuge in other countries.

William of Orange, who was in fact only Prince of an obscure principality in southern France, was keen to increase his status in Europe. One of the ways he attempted to do so was by marrying Princess Mary Stuart of England. Another was by acquiring hunting lodges and country houses in Holland and embellishing them and their gardens – and encouraging his supporters to do the same. William took an almost professional interest in garden design, and although Louis XVI was his political enemy he was deeply impressed by the French style and many of his gardens have some element of French decoration. Honselaarsdjik, near the sea, ten miles south of The Hague, had been one of his favourite residences since childhood. A hunting lodge in the guise of a castle moated by canals, it had parterres laid out by André Mollet and was only one of Prince William's gardens in which auriculas grew.

CHAPTER SEVEN

Monarchs, Duchesses and Painted Ladies

The Dutch have long had connections with British horticulture, but when in 1689 William of Orange, a Dutchman, and a garden-loving Dutchman at that, ascended the English throne with his wife Mary, the influence grew even stronger. As Daniel Defoe wrote in 1725, 'With the particular judgement of a King, all the gentlemen in England began to fall in; and in a few years fine gardens and fine houses began to grow up in every corner ... everyone with such a gust that the alteration is indeed wonderful throughout the whole kingdom'.

WILLIAM AND MARY

William and Mary both loved gardening. Mary, as a pupil of Bishop Compton, had no doubt seen many of the thousand species cultivated at Fulham Palace and may even have looked at the paintings Marshall did of them. Bishop Compton had been instrumental in bringing William, then Prince of Orange, to England and he performed the coronation ceremony.

In the Netherlands their glorious garden at Het Loo was the ultimate expression of their taste. It was Dutch in layout but French in ornamentation, and Daniel Morot, court gardener there, accompanied his royal master to England. William, who suffered from asthma, preferred to live away from the smoke of London and so moved to Hampton Court where he planned a garden to rival Versailles. Both Het Loo and Hampton Court were large gardens with magnificent embellishments, plenty of the fashionable 'greens' and the imported New World shrubs. There was a special emphasis on citrus trees with their

symbolic significance to the House of Orange. The florists' flowers were not forgotten however, and auriculas were grown in Auricula Quarters in both gardens.

Wherever she was, Mary wanted flowers at all seasons, and 'two or three bouquets for the service of her Highness' were made every week. Walter Harris was court physician to Mary, and at her request he wrote a book, *A description of the King's Royal Palace and Gardens at Loo*, which was published in 1699. Mary loved Holland and wanted this as a reminder of happy times, as she was never permitted to return there after becoming Queen of England. Sadly she died before the book was delivered to her. It confirms the presence of auriculas at Het Loo: 'In the spring there is a variety of the finest Tulips, Ranunculi, Anemones, Auricula ursi, Narcissus, &c.'

We also have records of auriculas being brought over from Holland to England. In October 1692 William acquired a collection of 120 plants from the legacy of Gaspar Fagel, which he had transported to Hampton Court via Honselaarsdijk. These plants, recorded in a document known as the *Hortus regius honselaerdicensus*, were mostly subtropical plants destined for the Greenhouse Quarter, but amongst them were a number of florists' flowers which could have managed quite well outside: tulips, anemones, hyacinths – and six auriculas. These are described as a brick red colour with yellow centre, a copper colour Double, a large-flowered purple with yellow centre, an ochre with white centre, a purple with a yellow centre and a purple with a white centre.

As well as in the Auricula Quarter at Hampton Court, auriculas were also grown at Mary's other residence, Kensington Palace. They obviously gave the Queen some pleasure in her short life. She died there in 1694 of smallpox, aged thirty-two.

THE DUCHESS OF BEAUFORT

One of the great British gardeners at this period was Mary Somerset, Duchess of Beaufort (*c.*1640–1714) whose gardens at Badminton and Chelsea were considered outstanding. Her London garden was situated adjacent to the Chelsea Physick Garden, of which her neighbour Sir Hans Sloane (1660–1753) was a patron. He was a wealthy physician and the owner of an enormous collection of antiquities that eventually formed the foundation of the British Museum.

Born Mary Capel, the Duchess came from a distinguished family and lived a full life in which politics in general, and the Tower of London in particular, played no little part. Her father, a staunch Royalist, was executed a few weeks after Charles I. Mary, who had married at eighteen and had had two children, was widowed when her first husband Lord Beauchamp was imprisoned in the Tower and caught a disease from which he later died. She had been widowed for six years when she met and married Henry Somerset who, like many others lived in exile during the Commonwealth. He, however, changed his religion and won the favour of Cromwell and so was able to reclaim some of his land including Badminton. Unfortunately at the Restoration in 1659 he too had been sent to the Tower for a short time. Finally her brother, the Earl of Essex, another great gardener whose estates John Evelyn admired, was, in 1683 accused of being part of a conspiracy against Charles II and was thrown into the Tower. There he committed suicide, by cutting his throat – although John Evelyn suspected that he was in fact murdered.

Mary, who had seven children and many responsibilities, ran her gardens like her household, with outstanding competence. In 1701 she engaged William Sherard, whose *Herbarium* I had seen in Oxford, as tutor to her grandson. Sherard was impressed with the Duchess's gardens, and in a letter written during his employment with her he wrote, 'In a few years they will out do any yet in Europe, being furnished with all conveniences imaginable and a good stock of plants to which I have added 1,500 and shall daily procure more from my correspondents abroad'.

Mary was one of a group of English women of means, often, but not always, widowed, who took an active role in their gardens. Mary in fact, came from a line of gardeners, her elder brother had created a great garden at Kew House where he had one of the new 'green houses' and specialized in myrtles and 'greens'. Mary also had a great stove house and an impressive collection of exotics from all around the world. She exchanged seeds and loved corresponding with botanists. 'When I get into storeys of plants I know not how to get out,' she wrote to her Chelsea neighbour Sir Hans Sloane.

Another correspondent was the botanist and entomologist James Petiver (1663–1718) who visited Badminton and found it 'a paradise of a garden'. He also commented on the Duchess's unusual type of 'Nursing care (which) scarce any Plant (tho' from the most distant Climates) can withstand'.

That she was, if not hands-on, at least very vigilant, is revealed in a letter from Sir Hans Sloane to a friend, when discussing the material he was collecting for his herbarium. 'Plants sent me from Badminton (were) very well preserved and flourishing there better than in any garden in Europe I ever saw. Her Grace having what she called an Infirmary or small green house to which she removed sickly or unthriving plants, and with proper culture by the care of an old woman under her Grace's direction, brought them to a greater perfection then at Hampton Court or anywhere.'

The Duchess's Florilegia and Herbaria

Mary's love of exotics did not weaken her passion for auriculas, which she in fact preferred to tulips. Her legacy to us in this respect is twofold. Firstly she commissioned a florilegium for each of her gardens. In the volume containing the auriculas

Facing page: Goldie.

Red Gauntlet.

the paintings are by 'D. Francom, A Servant of My Lady duchess of Beaufort's', and his story is both unusual and heartening. Daniel Francom was a young Gloucestershire man who was employed as under-footman in the house. When however, his interest in, and talent for, fine painting was discovered, the Duchess had him tutored by Everhard Kychious known as Kik, the Dutch painter working on the other volume, after which he was brought to Chelsea to record the plants there.

It was reported by Ruth Duthie in *Florists' Flowers and Societies* that of the auricula florets depicted in the Badminton Florilegium of 1710, 'One of these was a double, most were striped and one had green tips to the petals', thus showing an early move towards virescence. From the photograph reproduced in this work one sees no uniformity of petal formation nor of size, some pips being four times the size of the others. There is clear evidence of meal on the majority and a very good range of colours. They bear no captions and although there are some similarities with Marshall's auriculas, these are in no way idealized and, regarding the colours and striping at least, we can see some changes.

Auriculas were developing more colours, cultivars were being named and new categories were

appearing. The results obtained from seed were becoming less random as florists began to understand more about pollination. Richard Bradley (d.1732) professor of Botany at Cambridge and a pioneer garden journalist, conducted an experiment which involved the role of stamens and pollen in tulips. He also worked with auriculas, as this perspicacious passage from his *New Improvements in Planting and Gardening* 1717 confirms: ''Tis from this accidental Coupling that proceeds the Numberless Varieties of Fruits and Flowers which are raised every Day from Seed. The yellow and black Auriculas, which were the first we had in England, coupling with one another, produced Seed which gave us other varieties, which again mixing their Qualities in like manner, has afforded us, little by little, the numberless Variations which we see at this Day in every curious Flower-Garden; for I have saved the Seeds of near a hundred plain Auriculas whose Flowers were of one Colour, and stood remote from others, and that Seed I remember to have produced no Variety; but on the other hand, where I have saved the Seed of such plain Auriculas, as we have stood together, and were differing in their Colours, that Seed has furnish'd me with great Varieties, different from the Mother Plants.'

It was thus realized that it was the 'standing remote' and the 'standing together' which made the difference.

In 1721 Philip Miller (1691–1771) Chief Gardener at the Chelsea Physick Garden and author of two best selling books *The Gardener's Dictionary* 1731 and *The Gardener's Kalender* (1732) took this one step further when, watching bees, he realized that pollen was not spread by the wind but by insects.

Despite this the true mysteries of breeding were not fully understood by growers for many years. As late as 1820 even as eminent a florist as Thomas Hogg was instructing growers that if they wanted a 'pure unmixed breed of green edged flowers' it was necessary 'to remove 2 or 3 pots of any one fine sort in the spring before they came into flower, to a distance of a mile at least from any other Auriculas' and thus to 'prevent impregnation'.

Facing page: Prague.

The Duchess of Beaufort's second legacy regarding auriculas is her contribution to the *Sloane Herbarium* referred to above, now at the Natural History Museum in London. Auriculas are found in the first of twelve large volumes entitled 'The Duchess of Beaufort's Collection' and bearing the inscription, 'A collection of plants, most rare and some common gathered in the fields and gardens of Badminton, Chelsea etc etc dryed by order of Mary Dutchess (sic) of Beaufort all very well preserved'.

A VISIT TO THE NATURAL HISTORY MUSEUM

A visit to see the Duchess's auriculas was indicated. I made my way to the new state-of-the art Darwin Centre in the Natural History Museum, London, a futuristic cocoon-like edifice which opened in 2009 and cost £78 million. There, volume after volume of herbaria are housed in bright air-conditioned galleries.

I was welcomed by Drs Mark Spencer and Charlie Jarvis who had set out for me the large volume, No.138 which contains the Duchess's auriculas. These auricula pips, some sixty-five in number, were pressed around the time when the first Hanovarian King, George I took the throne, so not surprisingly they had faded. They bear names written in elegant copperplate and are contained in neat little hinged paper wrappers which one opens to reveal one or more pips glued inside. The majority, presumably those originally red, crimson and mulberry are now of a pale coral or amber colour, but those originally yellow, such as the large 'Lady Mary', retain something of that hue, as do the dark purplish shades like 'The Black Knight', which has frilly petals and the deep magenta 'Duchess of Beaufort'. Some striping is still visible on some specimens, and on most a clear ring of paste is still to be seen. Both the petal shapes and the actual sizes of the pips (1.5–3.5 cm) are very varied.

It was suggested by Ruth Duthie, a careful researcher, writing in 1988, that the pip of 'Sir Simon Harcourt' and one other auricula, showed the green petal tips associated with virescence, thus indicating a development at this stage towards the edged auricula. This was not immediately apparent to me, but armed with a magnifying glass, I examined the two separate specimens of 'Sir Simon Harcourt', together with another auricula called 'The Green Knight' and three tiny ones captioned simply *1713* and found that these did appear to have a shadowing of darker colour at the edges, a colour which certainly at one time could have been green although no variation in tissue texture was obvious.

Nearly all the auriculas in the Duchess's collection are named, many with aristocratic or topical names which chime with the events of the day. Sometimes a raiser's name is still used in conjunction with the cultivar name; in this collection we see both 'Duchess of Ormonde' and Oram's 'Duchess of Ormonde', but it is clear from the majority that cultivar names were becoming more generally employed.

Dr Jarvis then showed me another auricula herbarium, the collection of the Rev. Robert Uvedale (1642–1722) who cultivated a garden in Enfield. Although not very well known, he was enough of a botanist for Petiver to apply his name to a new plant, *Polymina Uvedalia*, which Miller retained in his *Dictionary* although it was subsequently superseded. That he was known to other botanists is confirmed by his assertion that he was assisted by Sherard 'in correcting my *Hortus Siccus* ... the turning over of, which gave him a little pleasure almost to his death'. Uvedale himself spoke of his herbarium as 'meanly furnished and most out of my own garden which cannot be supposed to afford much though it has been the grave of a great many plants which have grown there in half a century'.

The thirty-four unnamed auriculas from Uvedale's Essex garden thus give us an idea of the sort found in the more modest clergyman's garden at this date. In the main they seem good specimens and as well as individual pips of varying sizes and petal formations, one shows three pips and one has a dried leaf and a circular arrangement of seven yellow pips which is clearly pressed so as to replicate the truss.

Facing page: Shining Hour.

PAINTED LADIES

Amongst the named cultivars in the Duchess's collection there are two classified as Painted Ladies, Oram's 'Painted Lady' and 'The Royal Widow'. In their present state it is not easy to see exactly in what way these specimens differ from some of the other Stripes. This is because one of the chief characteristics associated with this type seems to have been an increased amount of paste, much of which may have disappeared over the years.

This is not, in fact, the first time the name Painted Lady has been encountered. A list of 'Flowers in my Garden' from 'an old diary dated October 1692' was quoted the January 1886 issue of *The Garden*. It contained the following plants in '55 auricula potts':

FROM A 1692 DIARY: FLOWERS IN MY GARDEN	
3 Dr Eeles	2 Striped purple
6 Blind's Painted Lady	14 Scarlet and White
4 Amaranth striped	15 Great striped brindle
4 Mr Andrews fine and striped	16 Large ruffled black
7 Fine striped brindle	17 Small brindle, Edwards'
11 Monument	18 Mr Borset's purple
12 Olive, striped	19 Double dark red
1 Blind's brindle	20 Painted Lady
9 Double stripe	21 fine Painted Lady new

Painted Ladies also occur amongst those sent, in 1704, by Jacob Bobart the Younger to his friend Dr Richard Richardson with a note, 'I now send a few auriculas which I think may be new to you; I being well satisfied that they are not yet in three places in England unless we reckon you're the third. They are put up in a box and are distinguished by these names, agreeable to the marks: 'Hellen' (a painted lady) 'Roxana', 'Cassandra', 'Rosimus', 'Cinthia', 'Bella Sylvia', 'Prince of Hesse' and 'Euridera'.

The Painted Lady is worthy of consideration as it was then on its way to becoming the most esteemed type of auricula in England, a position it reached by the first half of the eighteenth century, but unlike the Stripe and the Double, this category has completely disappeared. In his article 'Find the Lady' (edition 45 of *Argus*, the year book of the NAPS Midland and West), David Tarver speculates that in fact Painted Ladies disappeared because with the advent of the Edge they became irrelevant and were simply discarded. The genetic material however, must still be present in some plants, and it is probable that our modern auricula wizards are poised on the brink of recreating this type.

So what was the Painted Lady? It has been described simply as, 'so heavily dusted with farina as to look like a veil of powder on a woman's made-up face'. This would imply shading of pink or red and white. In fact the term has been applied to other flowers; there are Painted Lady carnations and pinks and even an old variety of red-and-white flowered runner beans still available today – and runner beans of course were originally grown for their flowers.

Expert Opinions

C. Oscar Moreton writing in 1964 described the Painted Lady like this: 'the whole plant seems to have been well powdered with meal. There is an eye of good paste and usually some meal on the edge. This is of various colours and these may be streaked, striped or intermixed'.

Allan Guest, a leading auricula judge and breeder today, included a photograph of one of his seedlings in his 2009 book *The Auricula*. It is an attractive, heavily mealed plant with red streaks which he feels, 'gives some of the impression of what the original Painted Ladies of the eighteenth century might have looked like'. He also cited Derek Parson's 'Hot Lips' as another example.

David Tarver writing in the current NAPS guide *Auricula History* says the Painted Lady was 'distinguished by the coating of farina which enveloped

Facing page: Basuto.

Hot Lips.

the whole plant, it included striping, streaks and apparent edging'.

These definitions are, of course by people who had, or have, never seen the real thing. One who *had* was Samuel Brewer (d.*c.*1743) a botanist and businessman who became gardener to the Duke of Beaufort. In about 1723 he wrote a treatise on the cultivation of auriculas and it found its way into the hands of Dr R. Newton who published it in the NAPS Northern Yearbook of 1954. In it Brewer said, 'But for the charming painted ladies (a class recently raised) that are all powdered in which their chief beauty consists they (are) soon by rains and dews disrobed of these lovely ornaments and deprive you in an hour of what you have waited a year expecting to see and admire'. He gives list of more than twenty auriculas including one called 'Pearson's Black Painted Lady'. The idea of a heavily mealed black auricula is certainly seductive.

Furber's *Twelve Months of Flowers*

A number of Painted Ladies are found in Furber's 1730 *Twelve Months of Flowers*. Robert Furber (1674–1756) was a nurseryman who had purchased some of the plants from Fulham Palace

for his Kensington nursery in 1713, when Bishop Compton died. His greatest coup however, was his *Twelve Months of Flowers*, a series of prints which depicted with great charm the flowers which bloomed each month of the year displayed together as in a great bouquet. Although dressed up very finely as a decorative work of art, this was in fact created with the shrewd commercial intent of selling plants. Auriculas had featured in British catalogues before – but never like this.

Amongst the earliest was the 1677 catalogue of 'seeds, plants etc sold by William Lucas at the Naked Boy near Strand Bridge in London'. This catalogue was discovered by the Rev A.C. Drinkwater, a vicar in Little Bookham in Surrey, in a small notebook which must have belonged to a former vicar who was setting out his garden. It featured auricula seed and also, in the 'Flower roots' section, 'auricula's double, striped and plain'. Plants and seed were also probably being sold at around the same time by growers like the Tuggies.

Fuber's *Twelve Months* however, was the first illustrated nursery catalogue to appear in Britain and the first to depict auriculas so stylishly. The delightful plates (which as originals or prints are still very collectable today) were drawn and painted by Pieter Castreels and engraved by Henry Fletcher. Each of the 900 plants depicted was numbered for identification and then listed by name. The vulgarity of mentioning a price was avoided.

The catalogue was marketed by subscription with a list of exalted patrons, the chief being Frederick, Prince of Wales and his sister the Princess Royal. The Royal Family were known to be great plant enthusiasts, so much so that it was reported in the *Gentleman's Magazine* that Sir Robert Walpole, the Prime Minister, had entertained 'Her Majesty, His Royal Highness the Prince, His Highness the Duke and the three elder Princesses to a dinner and dancing *in the greenhouse* of his mansion'. If kings and queens were happy to dine in greenhouses no doubt other subscribers to Furber's catalogue followed suit.

Facing page: Cornmeal.

About a third of the subscribers were women and included Mrs Pendarves, who later became Mrs Delaney, about whom we will hear more shortly. The cost was £1.5.0d plain and £2.12. 6d coloured – which, as £1.00 in 1730 was the equivalent of ± £85.00 today, put it well out of the reach of any but the wealthiest plant lovers.

The *Twelve Months* contains two auriculas in the plate for March, one of which is a Painted Lady. The April plate features seven more, of which two are Painted Ladies. Rather surprisingly considering the auricula's blooming season, the plate for August contains another Painted Lady; the plate for September two more auriculas, one of which is a Painted Lady; and even the plate for December features another two auriculas.

It is however, the fact that this important list of subscribers is edged with thirteen more auriculas which clearly indicates how very fashionable this flower was – no other flower is so well represented. All auriculas bear cultivar names, something shared in this work only by other florist's flowers. A number of the auriculas named on the subscription list show either patriotic undertones such as 'The Glory of England' or a bow in the direction of the exalted patrons, with royalty well to the fore: 'Potter's Queen Caroline', 'Prince Frederick', 'Princess Amelia', 'Princess Caroline', 'Prince of Orange'. In some cases the featured auriculas are named after the subscribers themselves, 'Lady Walpole', 'Earl of Derby', a sure way of catching their interest – and custom.

Four years later Furber published a book *The Flower Garden Display'd* which contained this same catalogue, together with another he published depicting fruit. This contains fuller descriptions of these thirteen most popular auriculas, written, it has been suggested, by Richard Bradley. It is these descriptions coupled with the illustrations which provide us with a vivid insight into the auriculas of the mid-eighteenth century. The plates, lovely as they are, were only hand-coloured after printing, but taken jointly with the written descriptions give us the very flowers before our eyes.

We read that the 'Royal Widow' auricula (which also featured in the Duchess of Beaufort's collection) sold for ten guineas (± £900 today), and with such prices it is hardly surprising that some nurserymen took advantage of the unwary.

Daniel Defoe in *The Complete English Tradesman* of 1726 issued this timeless warning: 'Thus, if you go to a garden to buy flowers ... if you know what you go about, know the names ... know the particular beauties ... when a flower is rare, and when ordinary, the gardener presently talks to you as to a man of art, tells you that you are a lover of art, a friend to a florist ... but if he finds you know little or nothing of the names of plants, or the nature of planting, he picks your pocket instantly, shows you a fine trimmed fuz-bush for a juniper, sells you common pinks for painted ladies, an ordinary tulip for a rarity, and the like.

'Thus I saw a gardener sell a gentleman a large yellow auricula,' he continues, 'that is to say, a *'running away'*, for a curious flower, and take a great price. It seems, the gentleman was a lover of a good yellow; and it is known, that when nature in the auricula is exhausted, and has spent her strength in showing a fine flower, perhaps some years upon the same root, she faints at last, and then turns into a yellow, which yellow shall be bright and pleasant the first year, and look very well to one that knows nothing of it, though another year it turns pale, and at length almost white. This the gardeners call a *run flower*, and this they put upon the gentleman for a rarity, only because he discovered at his coming that he knew nothing of the matter'. (So it's *Caveat Emptor*, as always.)

Holland, with its tulipomania, was not the only country in which florists ruined themselves financially for the love of their plants. It happened in Scotland too. James Justice (1698–1763) was above all a tulip man, but auriculas also contributed towards his downfall. Justice, member of the Royal Society and author of *Scots Gardiners Directory* published in 1754, was Principal Clerk to the Court of Sessions in Edinburgh and owner of a property where he created what was considered one of the best gardens in Scotland. It was well known as the site where the first pineapple in the country fruited. Justice went to Holland to study tulip culture. He literally spent a fortune on bulbs,

Facing page: Rowena.

AURICULAS IN FURBER'S *THE FLOWER GARDEN DISPLAY'D*

For the month of March, the first auricula is *The Royal Widow ...* one of the best of those Auriculas which are called *Painted Ladies*. With a good truss, well powdered it is marked with crimson streaks mixed with purple and some yellow and has a gold centre, it was raised from Seed by Mr Adam Holt a noted Gardener, 'and was so esteem'd that a plant was sold for ten Guineas' but that it is slow to increase but for that reason is strong because those which 'increase much, or put forth many Offsets, being weaker Flower-stems'. Next comes *The Danae Auricula* raised in Holland with flowers 'of a bluish Purpe stip'd in White' with a very bright yellow eye. (This description differs from that of one called *Danaee*, which featured in Trew's *Hortus Nitidissimus*, which may indicate that very similar names were used for different plants.)

The month of April, being the blowing season, has more auriculas than any other month. First is the *Glory of the East Auricula*, striped with carmine. It has a large truss, a good eye and 'is well powdered as any other of the Painted Ladies and is free to offset. Next is *Love's Master Auricula*. A (very) Double flower which is 'yellow stip'd or rather shaded with a dark Buff-colour, such as Dutch Pink'. This one will 'bear the Weather, for it has no Dust upon it to be wash'd off by rain'. This is followed by A *Double Painted Lady Auricula* which 'like the other Painted Ladies is well cover'd with Dust which makes the ground of the Flower appear white; this is strip'd with Yellow and a little Carmine Colour'. *Marveille du Monde Auricula* raised in Holland is next, 'a plain Flower, but is so fine a colour that it

looks like blue Velvet'. It is also commented that the Eye is white unlike the majority of Dutch auriculas which are generally 'yellow-eye'd without any dust upon them'. We then find *The Duke of Beaufort's Auricula*, 'one of the strangest Flowers ... because 'tis striped with Blue upon White, which none of the others are. This was also raised by Mr Holt and is a parent of *the Royal Widow*. The *Duke of St Albans' Auricula* follows. A 'good trussing flower with open blossoms and a good eye it is 'well powder'd, and stip'd with a Carmine Colour upon a Buff-colour'd Ground. The last auricula for April is *Grand Presence Auricula*, another Dutch plant with a great truss of flowers, large dark red blossoms and a large yellow eye which offsets freely 'but as it has no dust upon it, a Shower or two will not make it lose its beauty. (This, C. Oscar Moreton believed, would now be classed as a yellow-centred Alpine.)

For the month of August *Semper Augustus Auricula* is described. Another Painted Lady with a 'white Ground, strip'd with a reddish Purple'.

For September we find *Sheford's Hester Auricula*, another Painted Lady, yellow and crimson on a white ground, and also *Honour and Glory Auricula* which has a good white eye and is striped with dark reddish purple stripes on a white ground, so arranged 'so as to leave the edges white'. (Could this be an embryonic Edge?)

A further auricula appears for the month of December, the *Royal Purple Auricula* with a white eye which is 'of a pale Purple Colour strip'd with a deeper'.

and such was his mania that he imported not only bulbs (paying as much as fifty pounds for one) but also shiploads of Dutch soil in which to grow them. By 1767 his financial situation was dire. He could no longer pay his subscription to the Royal Society and was expelled. He took no notice and

continued to put FRS after his name and to correspond with fellow florists, but by the time he died he had lost his house, his garden and his plants, including, 'all the finest kinds of Auriculas ... hyacinths, bulbous irises and tulips that are in English or foreign Catalogues'. These were destined to be 'exposed to sale in Mr Justice's garden in Leith in large or small parcels as purchasers incline'. They ended up at a local seed merchants, and some were still available four years later.

Expensive as some auriculas still were, it must be said that the more ordinary sort could be obtained quite reasonably. For Prince Frederick's wedding to Princess Augusta in 1736 amongst the bills for wedding flowers supplied by Furber there were some auriculas at 1 shilling each, which is ± £4.30, similar to what we pay today. According to Mark Laird in his book of 1999, *The Flowering of the English Landscape Garden,* these were considered decorative rather than 'curious'.

Another superb collection of this period was that which the Earl of Meath had amassed at Kilruddery Castle near Bray in Ireland. The list, dating from 1730, names 230 varieties. Many of these are familiar from Furber's *Twelve Months*, and some are also found on the Badminton lists. We also find 'Blind's Nonpareil' which may have been raised by the same Mr Blind whose 'Painted Lady' featured in the 1692 diary previously mentioned. The Kilruddery list is divided into Irish and English Auriculas with some entries which have obviously been added later, for example 'auriculas from Mr Richardson' (the friend to whom Bobart had sent auriculas in 1704?) and 'English Auriculas from Hayter 1736'. We find all the favourites: 'Royal Widow', 'Glory of the East', the very popular 'Merveille du Monde', 'Duke of St Albans' and, of course, another 'Danae' (this time listed as an Irish Auricula.)

EHRET: BOTANICAL ILLUSTRATOR PAR EXCELLENCE

The illustrations in Furber's works are very pretty, and they give us an idea of the form and appearance of the auriculas of this period, but to see such plants at their very best we should go to the works of the wonderful painter Georg Dionysius Ehret, who showed a degree of skill and artistry hitherto unknown to England. His story is remarkable in that he rose from a humble beginning as a gardener's apprentice to meet and illustrate works of the

most prestigious names in botany of the day: Philip Miller, Linnaeus, George Clifford, Christopher Trew and Joseph Banks.

Ehret was born in Heidelberg in Germany to a family of market gardeners. When quite young he entered the service of the Margrave of Baden-Durlach (protégé of the Tulip Girls). Echoing the story of Daniel Francom, servant of the Duchess of Beaufort, it was noticed that the young gardener could draw. He helped with the plans for the new town and then began painting flowers for the Margrave in his spare time for which he was accorded various privileges. This however, caused friction with his fellow workers, so he left the Margrave's employ and went through various gardening, botanizing and drawing jobs before meeting Christoph Jacob Trew of *Hortus Nitidissmus* fame, who became a patron and a lifelong friend.

Ehret then found his way to France where, at the Jardin des Plantes, he met and learned from the King's painter Claude Aubriet. His next stop was England where he made the acquaintance of Sir Hans Sloane and Philip Miller. He also travelled to Holland where he worked with Linnaeus at the estate of the wealthy collector Georg Clifford. It was Linnaeus apparently who instructed him, 'to correctly depict the stamens, pistils and other small parts of the flower'. As well as illustrating the *Hortus Cliffortianus* in 1738, Ehret also illustrated the famous table of the sexuality of plants according to the Linnean system.

Returning to England in 1735, where after a slight setback at the Oxford Botanic garden (the unpleasant Sherardian Professor of Botany, Humphrey Sibthorp tried to relegate him to gardening once more – Ehret always referred to his past as 'those years of slavery' – rather than letting him draw and teach botanical art for which he had been employed) his genius was recognized and he was able to move freely in Society.

The Duchess of Portland (1715–85) of Bulstrode in Buckinghamshire, was one of his patrons. She was another of the energetic gardening widows who loved collecting natural curiosities, making improvements to her garden and, above all, 'botanizing'. She corresponded with botanists including Jean-Jacques Rousseau who collected seeds for her. She paid Ehret two guineas for each water-colour on velum he painted of her plants, as well as employing him to teach her daughters to paint.

Ehret married the sister-in-law of Philip Miller and stayed in England for the rest of his life. Much of his work displays a perfect fusion of artistic vision, scrupulous attention to detail and rare grace.

MRS DELANEY'S PAPER MOSAICS

One of the Duchess of Portland's great friends, also a widow, was Mrs Delaney (1700–1788), formerly Mrs Pendarves, whose name had featured on Furber's subscription list. After her first husband's death she married the Irish cleric Patrick Delaney and lived comfortably at Delville near Dublin, where she was never happier than when gardening.

In 1746 she wrote to her sister Anne that she was making 'a nine-pin alley' in 'a little odd nook of the garden, at the end of which is a very pretty summer house and in the in the corners of it are houses built up for blowing of auriculas'. A sketch she made shows the auricula houses which were pillared structures each with three shelves. After her husband's death she returned to England where she spent half of each year with the Duchess of Portland and also became involved in Court life.

Mrs Delaney was very industrious; she drew, she did shell work and she embroidered. According to her husband her hands were occupied 'even as her tea cooled', and through some of her exquisite handiwork we can gain a fresh perspective on the fashionable auricula. She embroidered her own court dress with flowers, and the petticoat (in those days this was visible) is decorated with embroidered lilies of the valley and the most exquisitely depicted auriculas which seem very similar in type to those decorating Furber's subscription list – which she may even have used as a pattern.

Mrs Delaney's chief claim to fame however, something which she only took up at the age of seventy-two, was her totally original way of depicting flowers in what she referred to as 'paper mosaics'. These were collages consisting of hundreds of small pieces of paper, cut out and carefully arranged so as to be botanically accurate and artistically pleasing. They became the talk of society and were even celebrated in verse by Erasmus Darwin (1731–1802), grandfather of the more famous Charles, in his poem *The Loves of Plants*:

… Delaney forms the mimic bowers
Her paper foliage, and her silken flowers
Her virgin train the tender scissors ply
Vein the green leaf, the purple petal dye.

King George III and Queen Charlotte, who counted Mrs Delaney as a friend, admired these collages and even had plants sent to her from Kew to use for them. 'I am so plentifully supplied with the hot house here and from the Queen's garden at Kew that natural plants have been a good deal laid aside this year for foreigners, but not less in favour', wrote Mrs Delaney in 1777.

The Royal couple, with the princes and princesses and a huge retinue visited Bulstrode for tea in 1778, and especially asked to see Mrs Delaney's *Book of Flowers*. The King brought over a chair and invited Mrs Delaney to sit. She, quite naturally, was confused by this Royal courtesy, but the Queen simply called across, 'Sit down, sit down! It is not everybody has a chair brought them by a king'.

Nearly 1,000 of these amazing collages, including five auriculas, are to be found in the British Museum in London.

Auriculas continued to find their way into other works of decorative art. Osterley House, a National Trust property near London, contains a chimney board, designed in 1776 by Robert Adam for Mrs Child's Dressing Room, which depicts flowers including auriculas arranged in a neo-classical vase. More are found in The Painted Room in Spencer House, London designed by James 'Athenian' Stuart c.1760 as a *Celebration of the Triumph of Love*, to symbolize Lord and Lady Spencer's happy marriage. The top frieze depicts alternating wreaths and swags of roses, poppies, anemones, guelder roses, tulips, orange blossom

Facing page: Joel.

and auriculas, which are attached to bows on hooks in the form of tiny gilt shells, all forming part of an extravagant spectacle beloved of the Georgians.

Auriculas were also a particular favourite of the designer Batty Langley (1696–1751) who wrote numerous manuals for builders, carpenters and decorators. In his *New Principles of Gardening* (1728) he suggests planting auriculas in terracotta pots which should then be concealed within decorative ceramic pots for use indoors.

Auriculas continued to be popular in Ireland, and they feature in the very unusual art of Samuel Dixon (d.1769). Dixon created embossed leather pictures featuring auriculas, but he also invented and popularized a new technique known as *basso-relievo* by which copper plate emboss was painted over with watercolour and heightened with gouache to give a 3-D effect. This was particularly suitable for natural history subjects such as birds and flowers. The plates were usually finished with black japanned frames and even now occasionally turn up at auctions where they are eagerly collected. Several of these paintings include auriculas and we find 'Royal Pair' and 'Dutch Triumph' which was also on the Kilruddery list. Echoing the work of Pierre Vallet in France (and maybe Furber in London) these images were often used as patterns for embroidery. In fact Dixon did not do the colouring himself but employed three young resident artists for this purpose. One of these, Gustavus Hamilton (1739–75) later became a well-known painter and miniaturist who also featured auriculas in several of the his works. These also doubled as embroidery patterns.

It is not surprising that auriculas found their way onto some of the exquisite 'botanical' china and porcelain being produced in English factories at this time. The Chelsea factory produced a series 'enamelled from Sir Hans Sloane's plants' in 1755, and in the 1790s Derby brought out a series copied from illustrations in William Curtis' *Botanical Magazine*. Auriculas were a favourite of James Giles (1718–80) who came from a Huguenot family of artists and decorated for Worcester, Derby, Chelsea and Bow. Some Giles pieces were exported to America, but sadly he died in poverty. In 2006 a rare teapot decorated with rustic figures, birds and auriculas on a turquoise and gilt background was sold by Christies New York for $110,000.

As the eighteenth century progressed great changes in garden style were taking place. The Landscape Movement became the latest thing, and although it swept many pretty old gardens away in its wake, as Mark Laird pointed out, flowers never completely disappeared. Running parallel to Capability Brown and his radical solutions, decorative flowers were still being grown in dedicated flower gardens and borders, often in geometrical or even 'flower shaped' beds. John Evelyn had observed and written about one such in Paris belonging to Pierre Morin, and in 1750 the proposals which Thomas Wright made for the gardens at Badminton included, 'The Duches's (sic) Flower Garden in which is design'd a Chineses Temple wing'd with Umbrellos to shade the Auriculas and other curious kinds of Flowers'.

It is also worth remembering that in order for Capability Brown and Repton to effect their innovative 'improvements', large acreages were required. The vast majority of people did not own such estates. Ha-has, hermits and ornate follies were far from the minds of the ordinary men and women who delighted in growing flowers.

Facing page: Sweet Pastures.

CHAPTER EIGHT

Edges, Stages and Florists' Feasts

The auricula, from its beginnings as the simple border type described by Gerard and Parkinson had, by mid-eighteenth century, come a very long way. It had been selectively bred to include a wide range of rich and splendid colours, some pure, some combined as vivid and intricate Stripes. Double and single forms of all types could be found, and Painted Ladies were valued for their colour and meal while in other, meal-free types, a shading of the petals could be observed.

Fashion, however never ceases to change. In the world of the auricula it was time for the next big thing. This happened just prior to 1750, when as Biffen commented, there occurred 'a series of extraordinary changes which, it is hardly too much to say, converted (the auricula) into an entirely new plant'.

GREEN TIPS BECOME EDGES

Prior to this date it had been noticed that occasionally a sport (an unexpected or unusual variation) would crop up bearing greenish tips to the flowers. Possibly many of these green-tipped auriculas had been thrown out as not conforming to what the grower expected, especially as their petals tended to be very pointed. Some florists however, must have persisted crossing them until better specimens, with correctly shaped petals bearing a distinct green edge, appeared.

Then, due to the amount of farina borne by the plant, an even more unique set of characteristics began to make themselves apparent. In those flowers with no farina the edge remained green, in those with light farina the edge became grey and in those bearing thick meal the edge became white. It

is this thick meal which has led to speculation by C. Oscar Moreton that Edges in fact evolved from Painted Ladies.

It was not until much later that research revealed that these tips were not in fact made of normal petal material, but were actually composed of exactly the same tissue as the leaves. The mystery as to why such a mutation, known as virescence, had occurred in the auricula remains largely unanswered although we now know it is a hereditary characteristic. Biffen's comments on the subject are of great interest. He discusses the complexity of the plant's possible genetic evolution and suggests a correlation between leaf and petal formation in respect of shape. He further traces back the meal-less Green Edge to the leaf type of the ancestor *Primula hirsuta*, and the Grey or White Edge to the foliage of the ancestor *Primula auricula*.

Although at the time none of this was understood, florists delighted in the new types that began to appear. That the date at which this happened must have been some time prior to 1750 is confirmed by the portrait of Martha Rodes (*see* frontispiece), which was painted in that year by Christopher Steele. The young subject is depicted wearing a satin dress, standing beside a table on which there is a large terracotta pot containing a very fine mature auricula bearing a truss of around a dozen grey (or just possibly green) edged pips. One point of interest is that the flower in the pot is presented face-on, but Martha is holding a similar auricula in her hand so that the reverse is shown to the viewer, thus affording us a clear sight of both sides of the flower. From the positioning and the lighting of the flower it would seem that the auricula is playing an important role in the painting. From the time of the

Renaissance, the fact that the subject of a painting is depicted holding an object or a flower always had an emblematic significance – remember Sir Thomas Hanmer's wife Susan holding a copy of the *Paradisus* in her portrait.

The other point of interest is that in the pot there is a marker or label on which is written what looks like a number, possibly XXI. Sometimes numbers or codes were used instead of plant names to deter thieves, but it could also relate to a breeding programme. I feel that here the brand new fashionable type of auricula is making such a statement in the painting that the Rodes family themselves may well have been raisers of auriculas.

This portrait remained undiscovered until 1987 when it featured in an exhibition *The Glory of the Garden* held jointly by The RHS and Sothebys, and to this day not much is known about the sitter or even who now owns the painting. Prior to this the emergence of the Edge was thought not to have occurred until 1757 when a Green Edge, 'Rule Arbiter' raised by the Northern florist Metcalf, was available in commerce. Another, 'Vice's Green Seedling', won a silver urn for a Mr Gillard at the Bristol Florists' Feast in 1771 and also a silver punch ladle for a Mr Joshua Springer at the same show.

Later, Isaac Emmerton writing in *A Plain and Practical Treatise* in 1819, describes 'Vice's Green Seedling' as a 'grass green flower' saying, 'it was much sought after and I have frequently been informed by very aged florists that this was the first green edged auricula considered worthy of notice and I have reason to believe this to be correct, it is a very choice and expensive sort'. He goes on to say he has no recollection of it himself but 'in my junior days my father kept it as a stage flower only but I have every reason to believe that green edged flowers generally took their rise from this specific sort.' Vice was known to have raised another, 'Royal Baker' which we can see from a painting by Thomas Robins the Younger had a narrow green edge to a mauve ground colour.

Another talked-about plant was the Grey Edge 'Hortaine', which appeared at about this time. The picture of Martha Rodes, however, is evidence that Edges had emerged even earlier – although

ironically, if it was a Grey, they were the last of the Edges to be recognized.

It did not take long for the ever-growing number of nurserymen to embrace Edges as the newest sort of auricula. Many growers were to be found in Lancashire in and around Middleton, the area in which Flemish weavers had settled in 1725. C. Oscar Morton points out that the name Heys as in John Heys of Castle Moor, raiser of the famous Grey Edge, 'Lovely Ann' was of Flemish origin.

Breeding and raising of plants continued, but as stocks increased values began to decrease, as is confirmed by an advertisement in *The General Evening Post* in 1756 for two very aristocratic specimens: 'To be sold. The stock of two fine auriculas one called 'Hague's Marchioness of Rockingham'; the other 'Ellis' Countess of Coventry' at a guinea each plant'.

Doubles too were going out of fashion at this stage. Painted Ladies and Stripes were still popular, but by 1770 the stripes had to be well defined and the contrast sharp. 'All colours as opposite as possible', according Hanbury, or as the poet Crabbe wrote of the auricula in his poem *The Borough*:

These brilliant hues all distinct and clean
No kindred tints, no blending streaks between
This is no shaded, run off pin eyed thing
A King of Flowers, a flower for England's King'.

The Edged auricula thus reigned supreme; as we have seen, on the continent it became known as the English Auricula. It was effectively to dominate the scene in England until the revival of Doubles and Stripes occurred in the twentieth century – and for some growers, especially in the North of England, it still does.

Of course not everyone was growing the aristocrats of the auricula tribe. The Borders which had been around since the days of Parkinson still graced many cottage and rectory gardens. That the clergyman Gilbert White (1720–93), whose *Natural History of Selborne* and *Gardener's Kalender* give a vivid impression of a happy middling way of life, grew this type at Selborne is evidenced by his diary for May 8 1784. 'Auriculas blow finely in the natural ground. Owls have eggs. The hangar most all green.'

Trouble.

THE BLOOMING STAGE

The advent of the edged auricula with its glorious farina, however, did give the florist added impetus to protect and display his treasures.

In the days of Gerard and Parkinson it was the custom to grow auriculas, which were then of the Border sort, in the open ground. By the time of Rea and Hanmer, when interest had developed enough for their colour and paste to be appreciated, a move was made to grow them in pots, and as we see references to the paste 'running' we can assume that these pots might have been moved under cover.

Doubles, Stripes and Painted Ladies began the long slow descent, which would eventually see them effectively extinct, but these too, carried meal, and so would have needed protection. With the new fashionable edged plant, of which the chief glory was the eye and rim of paste, however, this became crucial.

Further there is something about auriculas, especially when massed, which has a definite element of drama about it; they almost demand to be looked at, and the desire to flaunt them must have been almost irresistible to the florist. Means had to be found to do this effectively during their 'blow'.

In the 1650s John Evelyn had described 'benches and shelves *theatrically* placed in degrees one above another' so we may assume that even before the advent of the Edges plants were sometimes displayed on some form of shelf or stage. (Evelyn did, somewhat later, also suggest plants could be placed in a disused four-poster bed put in the garden, the curtains to be used for protection.)

It is worth noting that the word 'theatre' could at this time, have a somewhat different meaning from that of today, something more akin to a 'view'. Early atlases were sometimes referred to as 'theatres', and a book of 1718, *The Theatre of Dutch Pleasure Gardens*, shows plans for grand gardens.

In France and the Low Countries we have seen accounts of auricula 'theatres' such as those of the monks of Tournai which were in operation as early as the 1680s. No doubt news of these made its way across the channel, as in 1719 Richard Bradley was advising florists to 'set your pots upon Shelves, one above the other, in such a part of the Garden where Morning Sun only come … some covering must be provided to their Shelter against the Rains which are apt to wash (the Dust) away and destroy their Colours'.

In 1748 Philip Miller made a similar point in *The Gardener's Dictionary*, saying that when the auriculas begin to flower 'the pots should now be remov'd under some covert, to preserve them from the wet, which would wash the mealiness off the flowers … These pots are usually placed on shelves which are framed rising above each other.'

From then onwards we find descriptions for stages of all sizes and types. Auriculas were to be brought to the blooming stage just as they began to 'blow', there to be enjoyed to best advantage for the four to six weeks of their glory. The obvious benefit of having the auriculas at eye level was readily appreciated.

The basics were always the same: shelving within a protective structure. The shelving was invariably stepped, but the structure could be large or small; oblong, circular, pyramidical or even conical; collapsible, portable or permanent; static or in the form of a turntable. It could be situated outside in the garden or inside the house. The roof was normally of wood. The coverings could be canvas curtains (thus adding to the theatrical notion),

Facing page: Hawkwood.

wood or trellis. For the manipulation of these the instructions were often elaborate and complex. The siting was important: the stage should afford the plants morning sun only. Pots should be square pots or painted green and topped off with oyster shell.

Quite often the exterior would be decorated. 'As these stages are generally placed in some conspicuous part of the garden, many people have been at great expense to render them ornamental,' wrote the anonymous Florist of Bath in his *Treatise on the Culture and Management of the Bears' Ear* published in Bath in 1782. Referring to the French idea of decorating the interior of the structure with pictures of landscapes, 'This I can by no means approve of,' he commented, 'as their colours will interfere to much with those of the flowers. Let the inside of your stage therefore be painted in some dark colour that will serve as a background to your flowers and by such well-chosen contrast render thee appearance more beautiful and lively'.

Different designs for the blooming stage, blowing stage, flower-shed, bunker or penthouse as it was variously known, were offered by dozens of writers. James Maddock in *The Florists' Directory* of 1792 gave very precise instructions. Maddock (1718–86) who was said to be 'well known to the curious in flowers throughout the kingdom', was a Quaker originally from Warrington in Lancashire, the very heartland of floristry, who moved south and established a nursery at Walworth near London. Maddock had a son, also a James, who worked with him, and it has always been a puzzle as to which of them wrote the book as it was not published until 1792, six years after the death of Maddock the Elder. Samuel Curtis, a relation by marriage and a fellow florist, who published revised and improved editions at the beginning of the nineteenth century advertised it as being 'by the late James Maddock ... who was celebrated at Warrington', so it was almost certainly the work of the father.

This is what Maddock had to say about stages: 'Four rows of shelves in the form of a step but must not exceed five, the front or lowest shelf should be 2'5" from the ground, the second about 3" higher and the rest in the same proportion. These shelves should be 6" wide strong and well

supported.' He then gives equally detailed instructions regarding the roof and sides, and ends with the suggestion that a large looking glass be placed at each end, as this would be 'very pleasing by apparently lengthening the stage each way as far as the eye can see.'

Richard Bradley, Philip Miller and Maria Jackson in the *Florists Manual* of 1825 and Mawe and Abercrombie in *Every Man His Own Gardener*, described examples and illustrations appeared in several gardening magazines. In 1821 Rowlandson produced a famous caricature, *Misfortunes at Tulip Hall*, clearly showing shelved plant pots in the background.

Smaller Stands

Gardening was becoming a more popular middle-class activity, and pot-grown florists' flowers were easily incorporated into the smaller gardens. In the plans made by Richard Twiss in 1791 for a town garden in Upper Gower Street, London it is interesting to see that a small auricula stand was to be tucked into the rather unpromising setting of the light well, possibly for added protection and also so as to be visible from the windows of the house. We see a tiny sketch of the four stepped shelves of the stand 'to be set with auriculas, polyanthus ... ' at the foot of the plan. The stage would have been fitted with curtains, and collapsed and removed when not in use. In this sort of garden the owner might employ a gardener only once a month and so might do many of the tasks himself. Twiss in fact wrote to the owner of the Gower Street Garden, 'You will take as much delight in your garden as I do in mine'. At this time a selection of tiny implements including small water pots, little wire nippers and even a hexagonal hand glass were marketed for tending auriculas. One can imagine that this would have been amongst the owner's, or maybe his wife's, most pleasant gardening tasks.

That auriculas were enjoyed indoors when they bloomed is confirmed by a letter which, in 1776, Lord Edward Fitzgerald wrote to his mother Emily, Duchess of Leinster, from his house near

Facing page: Regency Topaz.

Blackrock in Ireland. 'We are enjoying the little book room with the windows open ... the plants are just watered; and with the passage door open the room smells like a greenhouse.' He goes on to describe how his wife Pamela 'Has dressed four beautiful flower-pots, and is now working at her (needlework) frame, while I write to my dearest mother; and upon two little stands there are six pots of fine auriculas, and I am sitting in the bay window'.

Such little auricula stands were made by some of the great carpenters of the day and can still occasionally still can be found in auctions.

A Theatrical Revival

It is interesting to note that regarding the display of auriculas the term 'theatre', which occurred in French, was not actually used in England until relatively recently when a new wave of interest, generated to some extent by the renovation by the National Trust of the auricula theatre at Calke Abbey in Derbyshire, ultimately led to these theatres being manufactured and made available again.

The Calke Abbey theatre is the only known example of an original design. It is believed to date from the Regency period and has eight tiered shelves in a large 20ft by 8ft, three-sided structure rather similar to a summer house. It would at one time have had pull-down curtains as, contrary to all advice, it faces south-east and without these would have caught too much sun for the auriculas to thrive. Now, when filled with the dozens of multi-coloured auriculas in bloom, it is a great visitor attraction.

Since the opening of this theatre in 1991 several other gardens open to the public, including Temple Newsome in Leeds, have erected their own versions. In London there are two small auricula theatres designed by The Dowager Marchioness of Salisbury, one at the Garden Museum in Lambeth and the other at the Geffrye Museum in East London. Lady Salisbury also designed one for the New York Botanical Garden.

Many private individuals, including Lord Rothschild who has a collection of about a thousand auriculas, now enjoy displaying their auriculas in their own theatres, and it is hardly an exaggeration to say that the interest in auricula theatres, which are now regularly illustrated in magazines, has been responsible for the upsurge of interest in growing the plants themselves.

FLORISTS' FEASTS

The florists' feast held at Norwich early in the seventeenth century appears to have continued as an annual event. Richard Pultney, author of a life of the English botanist John Ray, wrote in 1790, 'Mr Ray informs us that the people of Norwich have long excelled in the culture and production of fine flowers: and in those days, the florists held their annual feasts and crowned the best flower with a premium, *as at present.*'

During the first half of the eighteenth century we know from the painstaking work of the late Ruth Duthie, who searched through dozens of old newspapers and to whom I am indebted for much of this material, that such feasts were spreading right across the country.

By 1770 they had become widespread. According to the very exuberant Rev. William Hanbury in *The Whole Body of Planting and Gardening,* 'These feasts are now become general, and are regularly held in towns at proper distance, almost all over England.' The Rev. Hanbury (1725–1828) was a botanist and nurseryman who as a student had spent many hours in the Oxford Botanic Garden before being installed as vicar in the village of Church Langton in Leicestershire. Well known for arranging the first performance of Handel's *Messiah* in a parish church (his gardeners lined the street in uniform) he also set up 'plantations' of nursery stock from which he hoped to finance such grandiose schemes as erecting a huge Minster in the Leicester countryside.

Hanbury's favourite flower was the Bear's Ear, which he described as 'the pride of the English florist', commenting: 'While the Dutch are boasting of their grand tulips, hyacinths etc, we may lay claim to the greater honour in our improvement

Facing page: Merridale.

of these delightful plants, for the Auricula, if we regard its sweetness of odour as well as its beauty, must claim precedence.'

Auriculas for All

Commenting on the florists' feast, Hanbury adds a section from which we can learn several interesting facts. 'At these exhibitions, let not the Gardener be dejected if a weaver runs away with the prize as is often done ... A very small shower, which may come unexpectedly, when he is engaged in other necessary work will take off the elegance of a prize auricula ... whereas your tradesman who makes pretension to show will ever be at hand; can put his pots into the sun, or again into the shade'.

From this we can understand that by last half of the eighteenth century the auricula was definitely no longer the prerogative of wealthy or aristocratic florists. At the 1751 carnation show at Norwich, the stewards were listed as a sadler, a worstead weaver, a glazier and a barber. On another occasion a pair of millers were reported as breeding an auricula with 123 pips. Thus tradesmen and artisans could and did nurture auriculas, as maybe they had always been doing in a quiet way. By 1823, at an auricula show at Colchester the florists included a hatter, a leather cutter, a tin plate worker, a tallow chandler and several market gardeners. At this period the Exeter Florists' Society even advertised itself as 'An unostentatious Society ... composed of respectable persons and working men'.

It is interesting that here too is a reference to 'weavers', indicating a connection to the Huguenots who settled in such places such as East Anglia and Spitalfields, the very areas in which we find the earlier florists' feasts occurring. This gives credence to the idea that these gatherings may have been something they had attended in their home countries and had initiated in their adopted country. The London floral feast was established by Thomas Wrench, an auricula grower and nurseryman of Fulham. It is also worth noting that some of the descendants of these Huguenot weavers moved to Lancashire, where such shows became extremely popular.

An account of a feast outside London appearing in *The Craftsmen* of 16th April 1729 gives us interesting detail: 'On Tuesday last a great Feast of Gardiners call'd Florists was held at the Dog in Richmond Hill, at which were present about 130 in number ; after Dinner several shew'd their Flowers (most of them Auricula's) and five ancient and judicious Gardiners were judges to determine whose Flowers excell'd, on this occasion two Silver Spoons and Ladles were given to the Gardiners that had the best Flowers; a Gardiner of Barnes in Surrey was so well furnish'd with good Flowers that the judges in that affair, ordered him two Spoons and one Ladle. At the same Feast a Dish of Garden Beans with Bacon was given to the Society by a Gardiner near Leatherhead but he was by no ways entitled to the above by Plate by Reason he had brought no Flowers. The Beans were full as big as common Horse-Beans when out of the Shells'.

The advent of local papers, distributed throughout the county by 'newsmen' on horseback, did much to publicize these events. In Kent, another county rich in auricula feasts where they persisted until the 1820s, in an early advertisement placed in the Kentish Post, for a feast on 7 April 1736, it is interesting to see an odd phonetic spelling for the auricula, probably a result of journalistic inadequacy rather than local usage: 'There will be a Ricolus Feast on Friday 16th Instant at the Three Crown in Deal; every Person to shew four Flowers, and every Flower to have no less six pips; that Person who shews the most best out of four Blossoms, to have the Prize which will be a handsome five Pint China Punch Bowl. If any Gentlemen Florists have a mind to subscribe, they are desired to send their Names to the Three Kings by Wednesday the 14th and pay one Shilling, or to pay two Shillings and sixpence the day of the Feast. The subscription Money for the second best Flowers. Every Person that shews is to assert that they are, and have been his Flowers for three Months past.

N.B. there will be a very good Twelve-penny Ordinary.'

Facing page: Maggie.

Astolat.

The feasts were invariably held in inns, and sometimes the inn keeper participated by competing. The meal, the 'good ordinary' would usually be provided at 1pm. It could cost a shilling, two shillings or 2/6 although at one show, a 'brace of bucks' was provided and the cost went up to 4 shillings (maybe this was an 'extraordinary'). At another, the cost was 3 shillings and sixpence which entitled 'The Bearer to one shilling's worth of liquor extra.'

There were however, variations. At the Spalding Gentlemen's Society the shows took place in the evenings and no meals were served, only drinks. This society, which was founded in 1710, not only hosted shows but had its own physick garden and held lectures in natural history, antiquities and other matter of interest to the curious. Members liked to introduce new plants, and the minute book mentions a fasciated auricula with 107 'peeps' or pips.

From this minute book we also learn that the meeting began with the drinking of tea or coffee, but later in the evening 'a tankard of ale holding one quart and no more' was set upon the tables. Twelve clean pipes and an ounce of tobacco and a chamber pot were provided, as well as Latin and Greek dictionaries.

As the name suggests this was an exclusively male society – most florists' events were – the only women's names I have come across are those of the inn keepers. Spalding was unusual in that it was also a debating society; most were in fact the prototype of the competitive horticultural shows of the nineteenth century. They also have similarities with the shows held today by the sections of The National Primula and Auriculas Society.

THE SPIRIT OF COMPETITION

In all these feasts and shows the competition was fierce. In most feasts the auriculas, in their pots, had to be handed in by noon. Sometimes competitors had to pay an entry fee which went towards the next year's prizes. The exhibitor had to prove on oath that, 'the Blossoms are of his own blowing, from his own Plants', and in fact a steward would be present to ascertain that he had owned the plant for at least three months (if flouted, the offender could be expelled). Separate florists would judge the entries, and after judging, at 4pm, the plants were passed around the table for others to inspect and discuss. Prizes often went to a florist for 'seedlings of his own raising'. It was, after all, the production of new varieties from selected plants that was considered by Hanbury to be 'the glory of the florists'.

The prizes were substantial; quite often a silver ladle was awarded as first prize. At a 1750 auricula show at The Queen's Head Ipswich the first prize was a gold ring worth a guinea, the second a silver spoon and 'one ditto to the best seedling raised and shewed by one of the Ipswich Old Society'.

Other societies offered a copper kettle as a prize. Today at the annual NAPS Southern Auricula Show, a copper kettle is awarded to the winner of the Show Auricula Class and silver spoons are awarded for other classes – but these are only tokens, to be held by the winner for the year, whereas in the past the prizes offered permanent value to the winner.

With such prizes at stake it is not surprising that some people attempted to cheat. At one feast the flowers were 'to be dissected before the company'. This apparently to make sure no extra petals had been added. In Kent two individuals were 'debarred from showing any Flower at the next Auricula feast'. They had previously been the stewards, so one can only speculate as to what they had got up to. Sometimes several societies operated in the same town and rivalries developed. At one show in Ipswich the owner of the best auricula was to be entitled to 'a pair of salts if he is not a member of Mr Ryecroft's Society'.

Even worse than cheating was theft. According to Dr Dennis Baker writing in NAPS Southern Year book 2001, in December 1747 it was reported that 'about thirty pots of auriculas were stolen out of the garden of Mr Henry Miles, bricklayer of Canterbury' and informers were asked to report suspicions to 'The Florists' Club at Two Bells'. In April 1748 Walmer Castle also in Kent, was 'robbed of several posts of Auriculas, and several broke and spoiled besides.'

Sometimes it was convenient mention a reward for information alongside the report, as in the case of the feast held at the Saracen's Head on April from Canterbury.

Canterbury April 16
On Monday last at the Florists' Feast held at Mr Nye's at the Saracen's Head without Burgate, Thomas Saddleton, Gardener to M. Alderman Knowler, won the Prize with his Flower call'd *Cook's Godfrey of Burloig*. At the said Meeting it was agreed to give a Reward of Two Guineas to any Person who could give Information of those Persons who have been concerned in stealing Auriculas, within the Liberties of this City or who shall be detained in such vile Practices for the future, the money to be paid on Conviction of the Party offending.

Quite often a few months after an auricula feast a carnation feast would be held at the same venue, and there are records of silver rings, silver buckles and silver tea tongs being awarded at these.

There are few records of feasts devoted to other individual florists' flowers. During the second half of the century polyanthus and hyacinths were sometimes shown at auricula feasts, but the prizes offered were invariably less valuable. Tulip shows seem to have been restricted to Suffolk. It would seem that at this time the auricula and carnation were regarded as the true florists' flowers.

Florists' Feasts gradually died out to be superseded by more general flower shows but on 6 May 2001, to mark the 125th anniversary of its

founding, 'lady and gentlemen florists' of the NAPS Southern section met at the White Hart Barn, Godstone, in Surrey for a Florist Feast. They were requested to bring with them 'at least one pot of their best auriculas or Laced Polyanthus' to decorate the tables. The seven best auriculas were judged by Brenda Hyatt, and a copper kettle was awarded to the best plant exhibited. Then to the accompaniment of a pianist, a meal of cottage pie with cheesy potato topping, with a vegetarian option of lasagne, followed by bread and butter pudding or sherry trifle and cream and south Australian wine was served. The shilling ordinary by 2001 cost £15.00 a head, but the feast was voted a great success.

IRISH FEASTS

If there is little actual proof that the Huguenots were the instigators of the florists' feast in England, in Ireland there is no such uncertainty. The Dublin Florist Society founded in 1747 consisted of 30 members, drawn mainly from the clergy and gentry but also including several army officers of Huguenot origin: Colonel Chenevix, Captain Corneille and Captain Desbrisay. These were not refugees who had escaped religious persecution but officers who had come to Ireland to fight in William III's campaign and decided to stay on.

Auriculas, always popular, featured largely at the shows of the Dublin Florist's Society. Meetings were held monthly in the Phoenix Tavern, Werburgh Street, one of the most fashionable hostelries in the city. Dinner was served at 3.30 and every member had to bring a flower or pay a penalty of 2/6 (which was later changed to a bottle of wine). The plants were displayed on a mahogany stand, and after the names were taken, toasts were drunk to them. Carnations were toasted from July to January and auriculas the rest of the year. Occasionally meetings were held in the Captain Desbrisay's garden where a cold dinner would be laid on by the owner of the Phoenix Tavern.

The members sound a merry bunch. In May 1760, by way of a diversion, an evening party was arranged 'on the water'; members to 'meet at The

LEICESTER SOCIETY OF FLORISTS' STANDARDS

A description of the properties of A fine Variegated Auricula.

The Properties of an Auricula, are in Many Respects similar to those of a Polyanthus, as the Stem, Footstalk, and Formation of the Bunch, or Truss of flowers.

A Definition of the Petals, and their beautiful Colours, therefore remains only to be considered.

The Summits of the Pipe, or Neck of the Petals, ought to be vigorous, and fill the Tube with the Anthers, especially as it is destitute of that beautiful Fluting which the Polyanthus possesses.

The Eye should be a clear White, and round, without any Cracks, and distinct from the Ground Colour.

The Ground Colour is commonly a Self, and should be bold, and rich, and equal on every Side of the Eye, whether it be in bright Patches, or one uniform Circle, it should be clean at the Eye, only broke at the Outside into the Edging, a good Black, or Purple or bright Coffee colour, or rich Violet, are the best contrast to the Eye – a rich Crimson, or bright Scarlet would be most desirable, if well edged with a good Green.

The White or Green Margin, (or Edge) is the principal Cause of the variegated Appearance in that Flower, and it ought to be proportioned to the Ground colour, which will be the case if the Diameter of the Tube is one part, the Eye three, and the whole Peep six or nearly so.

All the Lovers of this Flower agree, that the Peeps should be flat, and ought to be round but this seldom happens to be the Case, falling greatly short of that most beautiful Heart-like form of the Polyanthus and we must be content, if is so near round as not to be what is termed Starry.

George. George Quay at the farthest 7 o'clock'. In 1751 Captain Desbrisay was appointed Chairman of a committee to award a prize to the gardener who shall raise best auriculas. £1.10 first prize, best ditto, fifteen shillings. The records for the society end in 1766.

SETTING STANDARDS

In the case of auriculas in the early shows there were no separate classes for different types. Richard Bradley in his *New Improved Gardening* in 1718 had given his opinion on what a good auricula should be like and had even given eight points of excellence, but this was before Edges had appeared on the scene.

The spring feast of the Society of Florists of Leicester in 1782 however, offered separate prizes for 'the best self-coloured' and the 'best and compleatest auricula' and it was the Leicester Florists, too, who in 1780 produced a document to assist the judges by enumerating the ideal 'properties' of the plant, in fact a prototype Standard of Excellence. By this stage the polyanthus had reached its acme of perfection and it is referred to in the following section on the auricula which appears to have been written by a polyanthus fancier. The auricula section is of interest as it offers an early description of the Edges (mentioning only Green and White Edge as the Grey was still not recognized at this stage).

James Maddock's *The Florists' Directory*

It was not until the beginning of the nineteenth century that classes for different categories evolved, and with this innovation the foundations

Facing page: Zambia.

for the Standards of Excellence we recognize today were laid down. James Maddock, whose *Florist's Directory* we have encountered in relation to auricula stages, set out for the first time a clear description of the relative proportions of the ideal auricula. When he did so it was the Edge that he had in mind. Indeed it has been suggested that the physical form of the edged auricula itself almost initiated the setting of standards. David Tarver suggests that the naming of plants *Rule Arbiter* and *Common Model* indicated that with these specimens the growers considered that they had achieved the desired proportions.

According to Maddock the flower is well proportioned when the diameter of the tube is one part, the eye three, and the whole pip, six or nearly so, that is, a ratio of 6:3:1. This ratio, which throws emphasis on the eye with its ring of paste, was challenged some years later, as we shall see, but was the one favoured by both Biffen and C. Oscar Moreton.

Maddock's Walworth nursery stocked a great number of auriculas. A catalogue, from which we can learn a lot, was published by Richard Weston in 1777. It notes the names of 313 auriculas, of which only three were Maddock's own breeding, which indicates that much of his stock was bought in. We see twenty British growers mentioned and find some familiar names like Cockup, Foden and Metcalf. That stock came from further abroad is confirmed too, as Weston in fact said 'Flowers are selected from the most esteemed and curious Dutch Florists', and one such is called 'Purple Kroon'. We also find a number bearing French names with no breeder's name attached: 'Cardinal de Fleury', 'Roi de Mauritane', 'Roi des Pourpres', 'La Belle Princess', 'Cramoise Superbe' and 'Roi des Olives'.

Prices varied. Quite a number were listed at one shilling each (±£3.15 today) but the most expensive, 'Pickup's Seedling' was a hefty £1.10.00d. (±£66.00). 'Georgian Siddus', 'Fellow's Defiance', 'Elfrida' and 'Hervey's Prince of Wales' were all at 15/- (±£47.00). Priced catalogues, which Weston brought out annually for Maddock, were quite unusual at this time. In the 1792 edition, 473 named auriculas are mentioned, of which forty-two are Selfs or Shaded Selfs and the remaining 431 presumably the new exciting Edges.

In *The Florist's Directory* Selfs are considered 'of no value but as common border flowers for nosegays' and it is also of interest to read that Maddox thinks little of the 'shaded' types which were so highly esteemed on the continent. The auricula, he considers, owes 'its present improved state to the assiduity and attention of English Florists to its culture who have from the seed of a flower imported from Holland about 50 years ago produced by continued cultivation almost all the varieties we now can boast. The Dutch and French have extended their improvement of this flower little or no further than to produce a numerous variety of yellow brown and shaded sorts greatly inferior to the beautiful kinds raised in this country'.

The Florists' Directory was very popular and was said to have gone a long way to reviving interest in florists' flowers. It was even translated into German.

Isaac Emmerton's Famous Compost

Just prior to its publication two other important books devoted to florists' flowers had appeared. In 1815 *A plain and practical Treatise of the culture and management of the AURICULA* by Isaac Emmerton (1769–1823) appeared, a work now chiefly remembered for the vile compost recipe. Composts, usually containing a high proportion of dung, were considered of paramount importance, and writers vied with each other as to the ingredients.

The compost which Maddock suggests seems positively fragrant in comparison with Emmerton's: cow dung, earth, leaf mould, peaty earth, burnt vegetables, river sand and decayed willow wood. This last ingredient was a favourite, as 'Such rotten Earth or Mould as is to be found in old decayed Willows' was suggested in Leonard Meagers' 1699 book, *The English Garden*.

Being furnished with such an old willow tree myself I intend to give Emmerton's compost a try. I also keep geese, but I shall not be following his advice to 'dig a hole in the garden 3 foot wide by 2 foot deep. Put in the hole two barrow loads of goose dung or (but not so good) pigeon's dung.

Facing page: Arundell Stripe.

Every week for 3 or 4 months pour over this one pailful of bullock's blood.' He suggests that it is wise to cover this with a hurdle to keep off the dogs and then says, 'mix well together until it has the appearance of mud or very fine mortar and let it remain in the hole until it becomes quite stiff, then add two barrow loads of fine yellow loam and three barrow loads of sugar-baker's scum. No sand is required.'

Emmerton's friend and fellow nurseryman, Thomas Hogg (1771–1841), author of *A Concise and Practical Treatise on the Carnation, Auricula etc*, the second important book to appear at this time, tells a story of how a young man in Stoke Newington who wanted to grow auriculas was persuaded by Emmerton to buy three geese for their manure. When the bullock's blood was stirred into the manure mixture however, the stench was such that his wife and his neighbours objected vociferously, after which two of the geese escaped, destroying the auriculas as they went. The third was caught and eaten.

Issac Emmerton was the son of another Isaac Emmerton, nurseryman (is there no end to these identically-named fathers and sons in horticulture?) who had also been a florist with a great love of auriculas – he is recorded as paying two guineas to George Metcalf in 1780 for a plant of 'Metcalf's Lancashire Hero', a very good Grey Edge which continued to win competitions for the next thirty years.

Emmerton the Younger ran a nursery and flower garden at Paddington Green. He had previously worked at his father's nursery at Barnet following his father's death in 1788, but he had to leave that district after a disorderly incident, possibly something to do with making an effigy of a parson and hanging it in a tree, possibly a matter of some debts, which landed him in prison for a year. While still at his father's nursery Emmerton *fils* had also become keen on auriculas. He competed but claimed he did not grow for sale. His auriculas, however, were outstanding. Even his neighbour, fellow florist Hogg who thought him boastful, wrote that Emmerton's auriculas, along with those of another nearby florist, Kenny, were 'unsurpassed for bold trusses, broad expanded pips of brilliant colours, strong stems and fleshy

foliage'. Emmerton was also an extremely industrious researcher with a great knowledge of his subject, and as well as hints for cultivation his book, which was sold by subscription, offered advice that (compost apart) is still valid today.

He also offers clues as to developments. Selfs were falling out of popularity: 'Fashion (I was going to say Folly),' he wrote, 'has in some measure banished these self-coloured flowers from our stages.' He mentions another type, Brindles, in which 'a kind of brown colour intermingles or variegated with bright yellow or fine gold, like a beautiful cock goldfinch on the wing', which he remembered as a boy but which were already almost extinct.

Of the Edges he mentions 'Vice's Green Seedling' which as we have seen he remembered from 'his junior days' as giving rise to all Edges, and also 'Cockup's Eclipse', which was held in esteem by London florists for its beautiful green edge to a violet ground and which was apparently an improvement of a similarly coloured specimen, 'Grundy's Cool Zephyr', which was too starry.

White Edges though, were not well thought of in the south although still shown in Yorkshire and Lancashire. 'Foden's Fair Rosamund' was a Grey Edge with a rich crimson ground, and it was highly priced at one and a half guineas as crimsons were highly regarded for breeding. Grey Edges were divided into Grey and China Edges, a term used by Lancashire growers to describe plants with a narrow silver edge to the outside of the petal and which there formed a separate class.

Other auriculas ranged in price from seven shilling and sixpence (± £12.75) for older varieties to two and a half guineas for some of the newer ones, and in the second edition of the book ninety-four varieties are listed. In spite of these high prices the auricula was no longer the province of the elite. The florists' feasts had made it more democratic and it was now the darling of artisans and miners as well as people of 'the more middling sort'.

Thomas Hogg's Practical Manual

Thomas Hogg's nursery was not from Emmerton's on ground now occupied by Paddington Station. Hogg in fact did a lot to help Emmerton both with his nursery and possibly with his book, for having been a schoolteacher before being advised to take up floriculture for his health, he had received a much better education than Emmerton. There was obviously some rivalry, possibly for sales rather than actual floristry, between Maddock, Emmerton and Hogg, who all produced their books within a few years of each other, and we find Hogg writing rather disparagingly: 'It is well known to all the old florists now living that Mr Maddock neither excelled in the culture of the Auricula or the Carnation although he managed Tulips and Ranunculuses well.'

Hogg was more of a dianthus specialist than an auricula fancier, but in his book, published in 1820 he gives cultural instructions for most florists' flowers. It is mainly a practical manual although he does include some rather whimsical elements, including a chapter called 'A Flower Christening' in which he says of the raising of a fine flower from seed, that 'the joy of beholding it is equal to a lord on first beholding the infant heir to his title, wealth and honours' and confirms that it is this which constitutes the 'undisputed title of florist among the brotherhood'.

He also gave an outline of the rules for the Florists' Feast of Islington and Chelsea, which indicate that they had not greatly altered over the years. He said that there were many other florists' societies in London but that these two were 'most numerous in regard to members but likewise most respectable being composed of amateur gentlemen florists and the most eminent public florists around'. He felt that considering the number of years auriculas had been cultivated in this country there were comparatively *few* varieties, but thought that more and better types were on the horizon because 'at no period has this flower been cultivated with such ardour as at present'. He noted several reasons for this: pride, competition and the wish of growers to 'have their name registered in the fancy-flower calendar'.

These books are of interest for the insights they afford as to the auriculas of the Regency period. Fortunately we can also see these flowers in pictures. In Robert Thornton's *Temple of Flora of 1812*, 'Grimes Privateer' the Green Edge, 'Cockup's Eclipse' another Green Edge, 'Redman's Metropolitan' a Purple Self and 'Egyptian' a Yellow Self, appear somewhat idealized and shown against an alpine background.

Robert Sweet's *Florist's Guide*

Although also idealized and presented with, as Biffen puts it, 'exaggeration of the formality of the flowers' a further set of twenty-six plates containing forty-two auriculas are illustrated in Robert Sweet's *The Florist's Guide*. Sweet (1783–1835) had trained as a gardener and worked in nurseries before beginning to publish this periodical from 1827 to 1832. He also cultivated plants for sale from his own garden.

The Florist's Guide is a most useful resource to the historian, as each auricula is described in detail with a note of the nursery from which it was obtained and the price. The work is in two volumes and gives an unrivalled impression of auriculas of the period. It features few of the disparaged Alpines; the vast majority are Green Edges, many with the favoured violet ground. There is also an Edge that must have been rather spectacular, 'Wild's Black and Clear'. Many of the names – 'Privateer', 'Smith's Waterloo', 'Wellington' and 'Hedges' Britannia' – reflect national feeling at this time when England was at war with France.

CHAPTER NINE

Auriculas in a Changing Society

The political and military upheaval at the beginning of the nineteenth century led to great changes throughout society. The Napoleonic wars began in 1803; Spain declared war on England the following year; Nelson died in 1805 at the battle of Trafalgar; and the British army was sent to Portugal in 1808 at the start of the Peninsular War. Wellington invaded France in 1814, and the wars finally ended in 1815. It is hardly surprising that the names given to auriculas – 'Rider's Waterloo', 'Cox's British Hero', 'Kenyon's Free Briton' and 'Gordon's Champion of England' – reflected a patriotic mood.

The Napoleonic wars had had a serious effect on trade, including the horticultural trade. As Emmerton said of the auricula in his 1815 *Plain and Practical Treatise*, 'about a hundred years ago the passion for this flower was greater if possible than at present. We had the credit then of supplying the Dutch florists with an endless variety of new sorts; whereas latterly we have been in the habit of receiving supplies of this plant every year from them, till the late war closed all communications between the two countries; and I have not yet had an opportunity to ascertain the return of peace with Holland, whether the Dutch florist cultivate it with the same pains and care as formerly.'

FLORISTS' IMPROVEMENTS

Emmerton goes on to say that the auricula, and he is here referring to the British plant, 'owes its present perfection to the care and cultivation of the gardener and florist … who have wonderfully improved many that were at first single and simple and have increased their variety, size and beauty to an extent which is almost incredible.'

One such florist, whose auriculas became known throughout Europe, had as a young man actively taken part in some of the momentous historic events. George Lightbody (1795–1872), was born in Falkirk, Scotland, a great centre of floristry. As a boy he joined the navy and participated in the defence of Cadiz and blockades in the Mediterranean, for which he won a medal. He also took part in the last American Wars where he acted as a spy, was twice captured, escaped and finally at the age of twenty-seven retired to his home in Falkirk where he devoted himself to auriculas.

Apparently his foundation stock comprised an auricula called 'Pope's Champion' which he bought for a guinea, 'Leigh's Colonel Taylor' for which he paid £3.15.0d (±£185.00) and 'Booth's Freedom', which cost him £1.10.0d (±£75.00). He then set about selective breeding. Towards the end of his life he considered he was doing well if he raised one good flower from a thousand seedlings. Some of the names he chose for his plants echoed his days at sea: 'Meteor Flag' and 'Admiral of the Blues' were both blue Selfs.

Such was Lightbody's knowledge that he was referred to by Charles Darwin in *The Journal of Horticulture* 1861. A reader, 'D of Deal', had written in with a query stating, as Darwin reports, that 'When Auriculas throw up side blooms, these keep pretty much to their character; but that when they throw up a heart bloom – that is from the axis of the plant, the flower, no matter what may be

Facing page: Butterwick.

Monk.

the colour of its edging, is just as likely to come in any other class as in the one it belongs to.' Darwin then added the comment that D of Deal was 'Corroborated by Mr Lightbody, (gardener and member of the Falkirk Horticultural Society Scotland, who raised numerous auricula varieties)' before concluding, 'This seems a very curious observation. It shows that some little light could be thrown on the laws of variation, if the many acute observers who read the Journal of Horticulture would contribute their knowledge on such points'.

It does in fact echo something Maddock wrote in *The Florists' Directory*, 'It is a curious fact that those sorts which are naturally possessed of a fine green on the edge or margin of the flower are often known to lose that property when the stem proceeds from the very heart of the plant.' He then goes on to call the side stems, 'the winter stems.'

'D of Deal' was in fact Henry Honeywood D'Ombrain (1818–1905), one of the many clergyman auricula enthusiasts. He came from an old French Huguenot family, and his love of auriculas dated from his childhood when they had been particularly fashionable. He lived and gardened for many years in Ireland before settling at Deal where he transformed part of a field into a garden. He made many contributions to gardening magazines; he was particularly good at imparting knowledge to beginners and was remembered as a very kind individual.

George Lightbody, too was apparently a kind,

courteous and delightful man. He had a friend and fellow enthusiast, Richard Headley (1796–1876) who named a Grey Edge after him in 1857, and in the same year George Lightbody returned the compliment by naming one of his Grey Edges 'Richard Headley'. Headley was an entirely different character from Lightbody, a typical country gentleman who never moved far from the village near Cambridge where he was born. He owned land, dealt in corn and had a brewing business. He loved sport and died after a riding accident.

George Lightbody lived for seventy-seven years, but the eponymous auricula lived for over a hundred. It was described by Roy Genders in the 1950s as 'A fine old variety but alas, it is now rarely seen. With its smooth paste, jet black ground colour and beautifully mealed edging, it was always popular on the show bench and though introduced in 1857 won premier award when exhibited at the Northern Auricula Society's show as recently as 1957.' C. Oscar Moreton adds that the foliage of 'George Lightbody' was 'Dark green without a trace of meal. The pip is large, free from cockling and with a beautiful light meal on the edge, some petals are inclined to be slightly pointed. The tube is of lemon colour and some of us would say too large but the proportions of the flower are exactly as to Glenny's rule'. (The cockling he describes is a wavy petal formation.)

GEORGE GLENNY'S NEW STANDARDS

George Glenny (1793–1874) was the garden writer who challenged the proportions of the auricula set down by James Maddock. He was a very influential figure; a prolific author and founder of the *Horticultural Journal*, The Metropolitan Society of Florists and Amateurs and The Gardener's Benevolent Fund. In an interview a few days before his death he said, 'Sixty-seven years ago I had a very fine collection of auriculas … I cultivated my stock at Hackney … From the observations and doings of the most successful amateurs I had become a very successful grower of the auricula … I had learned something from everybody and took many prizes.'

Glenny also affirmed that, 'the Bear's ear used to grow wild near London being extremely common and as hardy as the polyanthus'. While the latter part of this statement is true, it is harder to believe that auriculas of any sort were common growing wild near London.

Regarding the proportions of the auricula, in 1847 Glenny, in *The Standards of Perfection for the Properties of Flowers and Plants*, disputed Maddock's proportions: 'As in the colour and form consists the entire beauty of an auricula … I assert that, if it is to be done in diameters, the tube should be one, the eye two, the ground three, and the outer edge four; in other words, if the flowers were half an inch, the diameter of the yellow tube should be an eighth of an inch; the next circle, enclosing the white, two-eighths; the next circle, separating the ground colour and the edging, three-eighths; and the extreme edge four eighths. I have more plainly defined all other points; and it was only after two evenings' discussion, in which I urged various arguments, and showed examples, that my properties were adopted in opposition to all that had been done before, a strong proof it was different.'

Thus Glenny's ratio is 1:2:4. He also mentioned that the edge of the tube should rise a fraction above the paste, and his proportions make for a slightly wider tube. Nowadays the standards accept either system with a leaning towards Glenny. An excellent explanation of the finer points required by exhibition plants can be found in the NAPS Midland & West *Guide on Judging* by Allan Guest.

THE GROWTH OF HORTICULTURE

The British are world famous for their love of gardens, and the interest had grown steadily. In the sixteenth century some nineteen new gardening titles a year were published. By the seventeenth century this had grown to over a hundred, and by the eighteenth century to 600.

The growing importance of horticulture was signalled in 1805 when seven men met in Hatchard's Bookshop in Piccadilly to discuss the founding of a Horticultural Society (later to become The Royal Horticultural Society). The founders, who included Sir Joseph Banks and William Aiton, included representatives of different social groups, and thirty years later a woman was admitted as a Fellow.

Auriculas were still treasured by a wide range of amateur gardeners. The well-off Irish writer Maria Edgeworth, a keen plantswoman, wrote to a friend in April 1832, 'My auriculas are superb and my peony tree has 18 full sized buds!'

The tragic, penniless peasant poet John Clare also grew auriculas. His diary entry for May 1825 reads 'took up my hyacinth bulbs … made a new frame for my auriculas and found a large white orchis in Oxey wood'. In June of that year he wrote he had 'finished planting my auriculas. Went a-botanizing for ferns and orchises and caught a cold in the wet grass'. He also reports that he 'attended a meeting of Florists held at the old Kings Head, Newark last week. Prizes were adjudged as follows: Auriculas. 1st Prize, *Grimes Privateer*, Mr Ordoynd; 2nd, *Stretches Alexander*, Mr Ordoynd; 3rd *Wild's Black and Clear* Mr Welby.'

Clare, malnourished since childhood himself, struggled to feed his family of seven children, the situation not helped by the Enclosures Acts of 1809–17 which deprived the rural poor of much of their livelihood. Impoverished though he was, Clare was keen enough on his auriculas to have acquired a copy of Isaac Emmerton's *Treatise on the Culture of the Auricula*, on the inside of which he wrote a list of his other favourite flowers, the 'orchises'. Worn out by poverty and the rejection of his poems, Clare eventually went insane. One can only hope his auriculas brought him some joy in his hard life.

Auriculas were still inspiring artists and designers. The Swansea factory produced many beautiful porcelain 'botanical' plates between 1814–1822, painted by Henry Morris and William Pollard, which depicted auriculas amongst other flowers.

GARDENS FOR EVERYONE

Huge changes in society were taking place. The Industrial Revolution was beginning to transform

England. Wealth was now found in different hands. Daniel Defoe writing in 1815, commented, 'How many noble seats, superior to the palaces of sovereign princes, do we see erected by *tradesmen*.'

More houses of all sizes were being built and a very important selling point, especially in the suburbs, was a garden. Gardening had long been a British interest. As early as in 1180, writing in Latin, William FitzStephen, clerk to Thomas à Becket, in his *Description of London* had commented 'on all sides, beyond the houses, lie the gardens of the citizens that dwell in the suburbs, planted with trees, spacious and beautiful'.

In 1688 John Worlidge wrote, 'There is scarce a cottage in most parts of southern England but hath its proportionable garden, so great a delight do most men take in it.'

Gardening had become a national passion which filtered through every level of society, and as the population of England rose from ten million to forty million during the course of the century, amateur gardeners were becoming very numerous. The fashion for carpet bedding popular in municipal gardens was emulated in the gardens of suburbia, although later this was countered by William Robinson (1838–1935) the Irish gardener and writer who advocated the 'Wild Garden' style. Taking advantage of all these burgeoning markets, new gardening magazines for all levels of expertise sprang up, some directly targeting women.

Auriculas continued to attract devotees. C. Oscar Moreton cites the 1830s as 'probably the highest period of the auricula's fame'. He also points out that several growers coincidentally named a plant 'Ne Plus Ultra' indicating that it had reached perfection – and that effectively pride comes before a fall. The popularity of the auricula was certainly about to decline, but fortunately there remained a nucleus of sufficient serious growers faithful to its continued development.

THE DECLINE OF FLORISTRY

There were still florists improving their flowers and exhibiting them, but a collection of flowers was no longer a fashionable attribute. The era of the curious was over, and the concept that cultural status was enhanced by collecting flowers had disappeared.

Some magazines devoted to floristry were still published, but in fact the word 'florist' was dropped from later editions of Philip Miller's *Gardener and Florist's Dictionary*. Horticulture was taking over from floriculture, and with the exception of the Ancient Society of York Florists which had been established in 1768 (and is still operative today) many of the old Florists' Feasts segued smoothly into Flower Clubs or Horticultural Shows, their success assisted by the advent of the railways which meant that people could venture farther afield to compete – and indeed railway stations often had their own flower clubs which competed with each other.

The mechanization of industry was something with which the hand-loom weavers had not been able to compete, so many went into factories, taking their love of flowers with them. Flower Shows provided recreation for factory workers, and indeed John Claudius Loudon (1783–1843) instigator of the Gardenesque style, writing in his *Encyclopedia of Gardening* in 1822 claimed there was a florists' club in every town and village in the northern manufacturing districts. He in fact continued to use the term 'florist' in this work although he recognized that the concept had changed. Speaking of the auricula he said, 'A hundred years ago passion for this flower in England was much greater than at present' and added, referring to the tulip, 'now there are few good collections in private gardens of the higher classes. Like the auricula it is more the flower of the tradesman and operative manufacturer than of the botanist or man of fortune.' John Richards in his seminal work of 1993, *Primulas* confirms this, saying, 'The modern auricula is very much the invention of the English working classes.'

The cottage garden, which had been the pretty, floriferous surroundings of the *cottage orné* of the late eighteenth century, had developed into something of an idealized British fantasy that is still in evidence today. The real cottagers, the rural poor, for whom life was anything but leisurely, were

Facing page: Old Mustard.

encouraged to make their gardens models of productivity, and although flowers could not compete with potatoes on the list of priorities, they were still grown and loved.

The houses provided for industrial workers were small, with even smaller gardens, often only a cramped dark yard, but even so many a great auricula was reared in such conditions. The plants did not seem to mind the soot and smog of most towns, and of course the manure from the thousands of urban horses was keenly gathered for compost.

D.H. Lawrence, whose father was a coal miner, set his novel *Sons and Lovers* in the last years of the nineteenth century. He describes the miner's dwellings as consisting of two blocks where, 'in the little front gardens are auriculas and saxifrage in the shadow of the bottom block, sweet williams and pinks in the sunny top block.'

The auriculas Lawrence refers to however, were not the aristocratic show types developed so patiently by the florists, for all the while the refinements were taking place in Show Auriculas, examples of the old Border types were flourishing happily in cottage gardens – where many are still to be found today.

BORDERS: THE COUNTRY COUSINS

Although the Borders are often considered the country cousin of the show types, in fact those aristocrats, as is often the case in human life, owe their origins to the more humble stock. We read that the classification of a Border is 'imprecise … and includes a wide range of varied ancestry … the general form being somewhat reminiscent of the wild *P. Auricula*' or that 'this class is sometimes infiltrated by failed Selfs and Alpines too nice to throw away but no longer welcome amongst their near relatives.'

As we have seen the genetic potential of the auricula is rich, and its categorization according to strict Standards of Excellence is only a man-made construct towards which florists consciously develop their seedlings. Borders are to some extent the ones which escaped this discipline and so

developed more randomly and it must be said, sometimes more vigorously.

Interest in this type however, has increased recently as it is recognized that they have the longest and strongest links with the past and are thus living antiques to be treasured. Traditionally even a pin-eyed flower is acceptable in the Border category. Even in 1815 Emmerton said, 'pin eyed flowers will do well for the flower borders and will there make a shew and serve to cut for nosegays'. 'George Swinford's Leathercoat' and several other lovely Borders are indeed pin-eyed.

Borders, in fact are the only category in which a pin-eye (that is, a plant in which the style and stigma protrude from the middle of the tube) is acceptable in show classes. All other categories must be thrum-eyed (showing the stamens and anthers at the top of the tube). It is strange how that this seemingly arbitrary requirement was universally adopted by connoisseurs both in England and on the continent. The apparent reasoning was that the pin eye gives a 'meagre and empty' effect and that the symmetry of the little bunch of stamens which form the thrum is simply more beautiful. Symmetry was part of the aesthetic of the period when the auricula was at the pinnacle of its popularity, so this does make sense.

Many Borders are deliciously scented, and for this reason I have pots of them in my greenhouse – entering which on a spring morning is one of life's great pleasures. They do, however, also thrive outside in the garden.

Old Country Names

For generations these plants were simply referred to as *riclous, ricklers, riclasses, recklesses* and other variations thereof. We read a 1714 entry in Nicholas Blundell's diary *The Great Diurnal* which he kept for twenty-five years, 'I helped John Bannister set a great many roots of Euriculases in the Knot'. In 1722 he again made an entry, 'I went to Ailes Mellins to look at her Ariculases'. His spelling did however, settle down somewhat as by 1724 he

Facing page: Cortina.

Moselle.

wrote: 'I put some compost in my Flower Pots in order to plant Auriculas in them'.

Some of the older names were still in use within living memory. It was reported in Derek Tarver's *Auricula Miscellany* that an old lady visiting Calke Abbey's Plant Fair, on seeing the auriculas said, 'My old dad used to call them *ricklearses*.'

In D.H. Lawrence we find a somewhat unexpected reference to them in *Lady Chatterley's Lover* which is set in the 1920s. Connie, Lady Chatterley, is visiting Mrs Flint, a farmer's wife. 'Connie emerged in the farm's little front garden, shut by a privet hedge. There were two rows of auriculas by the path, very velvety and rich. "Lovely auriculas," said Connie. "*Reckless*, as Luke called them," laughed Mrs Flint, "Have some"'. So Lady Chatterley goes off to meet her lover carrying the 'velvet and primrose flowers'.

We also sometimes come across them referred to as 'Baziers', which is surely a corruption of Bear's Ears. Alice E. Coats in *Flowers and their Histories* 1956 suggests that 'bazier' derives from 'bizarre', but as the word 'bizarre' has more often referred to a Stripe, it is seems unlikely. 'Auriculas,' according to Eleanour Sinclair Rohde in her 1931 book *The Scented Garden*, 'in later years became especially popular with the Lancashire weavers who called the flowers "Baziers",' and she quotes and an old Lancashire song:

Come listen awhile unto what we shall say,
Concerning the season, the month we call May;
For the flowers they are springing, and the birds
   they do sing,
And the baziers are sweet in the morning of May.
When the trees are in bloom, and the meadows
   are green,
The sweet-smelling cowslips are plain to be seen;
The sweet ties of nature, which we plainly do see,
For the baziers are sweet in the morning of May.

'Maying' according to an elderly correspondent in *Chambers Book of Days*, was a South Lancashire rural custom whereby four to six men went singing songs from mid April until May, as a charm to drive winter away.

Eleanour Sinclair Rohde also said, 'The old names still survive in different parts of the country. In Gloucestershire they used to call them Vanner's or Venner's Aprons'. Vanners wore leather aprons so could this be a reference to Leathercoats?' Leathercoats however, make up only a small proportion of the Border types and David Tarver suggests that Venner's Aprons is a Gloucestershire corruption of Venus' Apron.

There is a group of older Borders, usually with flowers of muted colours and deeply mealed leaves, which have long been known as 'Dusty Millers' or 'Old Dusty Millers'. Other Borders are just prefixed with 'Old' as in 'Old Clove Red' and 'Old Suffolk Bronze'.

There is still something very seductive about the idea of coming across some of these old, half-forgotten flowers in cottage gardens. We read that 'Broadwell Gold' was discovered by Joe Elliott in a Cotswold garden; that Ruth Duthie found 'George Swinford's Leathercoat' at Filkins, the Oxford garden of a Mr G. Swinford; at East Lambrook 'The Duke of Edinburgh' was grown by Margery Fish, who thought it of Irish origin.

It would seem that a number of good old Borders originated from Ireland, several cultivated by the legendary Miss Wynne of Avoca who grew not only 'Osborne's Green', named after the owner of the cottage in which it was found, but also 'Mrs

Facing page: Helen Barter.

Dargan'. 'Old Irish Scented', another lovely plant, hailed from Lissadel in County Sligo where the Gore-Booth family ran a nursery, long after two of the Gore-Booth sisters were immortalized by W.B. Yeats in a poem as 'Two girls in silk kimonos, both beautiful, one a gazelle.' It is possible that another good yellow, 'Queen Alexandra', also came from Lissadel.

Scotland too, was fertile ground for old Borders. Mary McMurtrie, who died in 2003 at the age of 101, painted several from the garden of Balbithan, the old Scots fortified house she restored. These can now be seen in a book by Timothy Clark, *Mary Mcmurtrie's Country Garden Flowers*. 'Craig Dhu' and 'Craig Nordie', both illustrated therein, are old varieties found in the 1940s in a garden in Glen Muick by Alex Duguid and named after two Deeside hills.

Although these old varieties, many of which are still available today, are a tangible link with history, some excellent new ones are being bred, including the vivid 'Dales Red' and the lovely 'Old Fashioned', which – in spite of looking as if it would be quite at home in a British cottage garden – was fact was bred by Herb Dixon in America and came to England via Maedyth Martin.

Facing page: Serenity.

CHAPTER TEN

Auriculas Travel to the New World

In Europe in the nineteenth century, as we saw in Chapter 2, the most important news in the history of the auricula was the discovery which Anton Kerner von Marilaun made about the ancestry of the plant. Of this, Dr Georg Gärtner of Innsbruck Botanical Institute, wrote in 2004, 'Kerner's unbroken interest in the question of hybridization and fertility was focused on the hybrid of *Primula auricula* and *P. hirsuta* discovered in the Tirol known as *Primula pubescens* in literature. This as Kerner convincingly established, was the beginning of the garden primula which today is found in many forms in commerce and which in Kerner's time was found in many Tyrolean farm gardens.'

CONTINENTAL INTEREST WANES

Generally however, on the continent auriculas were becoming less popular, and as the nineteenth century came to an end breeding of the finer types was undertaken less and less. Floriculture, as it had been practised, was all but over, and gardeners were coming to rely on commercial nurseries for the bulk of their horticultural requisites.

According to his memoirs, Georg Arends (1863–1952) the well-known German expert on herbaceous plants who saw auriculas in England in the 1890s, considered them too weak for the cut flower trade, especially in view of the competition of the commercially grown primulas.

Seeds continued to be offered until the Second World War, but the days of the aristocrats were over – until that is, the second half of the twentieth century when auriculas in Germany experienced something of a renaissance. For the last twelve years an auricula weekend devoted to Goethe's favourite flowers has been held in the Long Room of the Orangerie of Belvedere Castle. There, specialist growers Frederick Moye and Werner Hoffmann display, sell and swap auriculas from their collections of over 900 sorts, many of their own raising.

In France on the eve of the Revolution, while the population went hungry the elite continued to adorn themselves. *La Toilette de Flore – An Essay on Plants and Flowers Used to Adorn Ladies*, by Pierre Buc'hoz (1731–1807), which was published in 1784, is effectively a book of beauty tips with sections devoted to plant-based balms, lotions and unguents to whiten teeth, eliminate wrinkles and dye grey hair. It also deals with the creation of small floral posies: a flat 'trimming bouquet' pinned along the edge of a low neckline could, it is suggested, combine pansies, larkspur, anemones, buttercup and Bear's Ears – the latter highly prized because of their lasting quality. Other little posies could be worn in the hair, and an aristocratic lady recounts how she placed in her *coiffure* a tiny glass bottle of water, 'something very much in fashion but rather uncomfortable', into which the stems of the flowers were inserted to keep them fresh.

After the French Revolution a change in the perception of florists' flowers took place. The excesses of the *Ancien Regime* had become associated with corruption, and although flowers themselves did not go out of fashion, in order to be politically correct showy flowers had to be avoided. What

Facing page: Midnight.

changed as a result was that plants became democratized and 'curious' flowers became available to a larger circle. The flower markets did good business, and plants in clay pots, boxes, containers in window boxes bloomed all over Paris as well as in the beds and borders of country *jardins de cure*.

Florists' flowers by no means died out; they simply got lost in the crowd. Before doing so however, bear's ears were still treasured in some high places. Napoleon loved violets and Josephine adored roses but she was also passionate about many other flowers. On a flower supplier's invoice found at Chateau Malmaison, amongst the roses, jasmine, lilac, pinks, carnations, ranunculus and *fleurs du champs* ordered for the Empress's head dresses, we find a *Coiffure en Oreilles d'Ours* costing 72 francs. Auriculas are also featured in *Le Tombeau de Julie* by Van Dael, a painting which was in fact purchased by Empress Josephine who also owned some of the paintings of Pierre Joseph Redouté (1759–1840), famous for his roses but who also depicted auriculas.

THOMAS JEFFERSON: AURICULAS IN THE NEW WORLD

Someone who was walking those pre-Revolution Paris streets, buying plants of 'carnations, auriculas, tuberoses &c' from the French markets, was Thomas Jefferson (1743–1826) American Envoy to France and future US President. Jefferson was a plant enthusiast who as a young man had sown auricula seeds at his childhood home, Shadwell in Virginia.

It is possible that arriving in Paris in 1785 and moving in elite circles he encountered some of the *curieux fleuristes*. Certainly in 1803 he wrote to Madame Noailles de Tesse saying, 'when I return to Monticello I believe I shall become a florist'. Monticello was the classical mansion he had had built and for which, armed with his 1768 copy of Miller's *Gardener's Dictionary*, he planned the magnificent gardens which are detailed in his own *Garden Book*, a diary which he kept from 1766 to 1824. There are many mentions of auriculas both in this book and in his correspondence.

His garden mentor, with whom much of this correspondence is conducted, was Bernard McMahon (1775–1816) pioneer American horticulturalist (commemorated by the shrub *Mahonia*) who as well as advising Jefferson, grew seeds collected for the President by plant hunters. McMahon published the very influential *The American Gardener's Calender* in 1806, before purchasing land and creating his own nursery, which he called Upsal in memory of Linnaeus' garden at Uppsala.

Between 1767 and 1813 Jefferson makes some ten references to auriculas, but one gets the impression that they did not really thrive. The Virginian climate was not favourable, and there were difficulties in obtaining supplies. 'Of Auriculas we have none here worth a cent', wrote MacMahon, adding, 'I expect some good ones from London this spring, if they come safe, you shall have a division next season.' The implication here is that Jefferson requires specific plants, and indeed in 1812 there is another reference to '6 pots of auriculas, different kinds', but seed is also received on several occasions.

Auriculas in these early days were obviously imported, mainly from England. Some plants must have grown on, undisturbed in gardens in favourable climatic zones for many years. Indeed they were amongst the flowers listed when New York State designed a model garden for the 1893 World Columbian Exposition in Chicago. The theme was 'An Old-Fashioned New York Garden' and, according to the report of the General Managers, amongst the plants, all sourced from old gardens were: 'phlox, larkspur, Jacob's ladder, hearts ease, wall flowers, polyanthus and auriculas … all cherished acquaintances of a floral past'. From the company of old-fashioned cottage garden flowers the auriculas are keeping in this list, it seems likely that these were Border types.

PACIFIC NORTHWEST: THE IDEAL CLIMATE

In the twentieth century, in the New World the number of auricula growers gradually increased

Facing page: Coffee.

in spite of climate difficulties in much of the country. Oregon had a particularly kind climate, however, and Florence Bellis, founder of the famous Barnhaven Primroses nursery and editor of the American Primrose Society's Journal for many years, counted amongst the enthusiasts of the 1920s a group of people who began to import seed of Show and Alpine types: Lou Roberts, Audra Link and the garden columnist, Carl Maskey, all of Milwaukie, Oregon. Dr W. Blasdale, author of *The Cultivated Species of Primula*, also raised Shows and Alpines, but it was a struggle as he lived in sunny California. In the 1930s Mrs Rae Berry, also in Oregon, raised Show Auriculas, including one she called 'Snow Lady' from seed obtained from a British source. The American Primrose Society was founded in Oregon in 1941, and interest in hybridizing began to take off. It was not an opportune moment for obtaining stocks, however, as in England food production was a priority and nurseries were at a low ebb.

After the war things gradually picked up, and contact was established between APS members and British growers via the NAPS. Florence Bellis commissioned articles for the APS Journal from British growers such as Dan Bamford and Cyril Haysom, and Dan Bamford subsequently presented the famous Copper Kettle for the best Show auricula. British growers also offered advice which, in the opinion of Gwen Baker, was not always entirely helpful as it tended to impose exactly the same standards on American as English auriculas and thus slowed down progress.

By the 1950s the largest grower, Mrs Ella Torpen of Oregon, had built up good stocks. Both she and Robert Saxe of California came to England in order to see plants, meet growers and visit shows. In Canada meanwhile, further stocks of good plants were being made available by Mr Frank Michaud of British Columbia, who had imported his foundation plants from Cyril Haysom. His nursery Alpenglow, was a mecca for auricula enthusiasts at the time.

In 1963 Cyrus Happy III of Tacoma Washington, one of the most prominent American growers, registered the first Alpine auricula, a gold centre which was named 'Golden Girl'. Cy Happy also hybridized Green Edges and Doubles. After reading an article 'An Old Irish Garden' by C. Oscar Moreton in the NAPS Northern Year book in the 1950s, he began a correspondence with the Irish primula enthusiast, Miss Wynne of Avoca. He mentioned that he was interested in Doubles, some of which he had been growing from seed. Doubles were very rare in Europe at that time, but Miss Wynne still had a few old varieties and she sent Cy Happy a floret of 'Mrs Dargan', the pollen of which he used in an attempt to recreate the striped Double. He did in fact achieve something unexpected – not a Stripe, but a Double, each petal of which was dusted with farina, which he called 'Dusty Doubles'. Later from a 'Dusty Double' and 'Old Irish Green', another of his seedlings, a series of Striped Doubles did emerge.

Herb Dickson was a friend of Cy's, and together they put on the Tacoma Primrose Show. Known as 'Mr Primrose', Herb ran a nursery at Chehalis, Washington. When he retired, his friend April Boettgar took over his stock, and it was she who spotted a Border which she called 'Old Fashioned', a chance seedling which Herb had probably grown from seed and which Maedyhte Martin subsequently brought over to the UK.

Two other raisers who made great contributions to the development of the auricula, in particular the Double, were Mrs Denna Snuffer and Ralph Balcom. By careful hybridizing and subsequent export of plants and seeds to England, they are to be credited with the important matter of facilitating the revival of Doubles in this country.

MAEDYTHE MARTIN: MODERN HYBRIDIZER

Nowadays one of the most lively New World hybridizers is the Canadian Maedythe Martin from Vancouver, who is known to many British enthusiasts as she visits auricula friends and attends the Annual General Meetings over here. She learned the knack of pollinating auriculas from Cy Happy and is currently working on Stripes, having been inspired by Allan Hawkes in 1996. Starting with the limited plant material available, she now has a range of Stripes, some semi-double. Plants and seed from Derek Salt have resulted in a strain of

Doubles. She says that odd things have shown up, some with lots of meal, which hopefully may result in some Painted Ladies – prototypes are in place already.

One other grower in Victoria, Bryan Davies, has used pollen from Maedythe's plants over the past five years and now has a surprisingly good variety of Shows and Stripes. There are not many serious auricula growers in North America, but the few who are there seem to find each other. Ian MacGowan on Whidbey Island in Washington State has a broad range of Show plants now, thanks to the generosity of Les Allen. Susan Schnare in New Hampshire has a collection of named auriculas, largely from England. These growers correspond regularly, particularly in spring, and visit when possible.

The greatest challenge for North American growers has always been finding the right conditions for Show Auriculas, but they are a resourceful bunch and their budding collections are a source of joy and pride every bit the equal of the 'curious' of the past on this side of the Atlantic.

It is also of interest to note that auriculas have been an inspiration to American designers. In 1938 the Picart China Company marketed a beautiful hand-painted dinner service depicting auriculas. That interest continues today. Vladimir Kanevsky from New Jersey, who loves auriculas, creates refined and life-like flowers in porcelain and tôle. His pair of yellow auriculas presented in antique pots are of such charm and delicacy that they would not have been out of place on Louis XIV's mantelpiece.

Marmion.

CHAPTER ELEVEN

Towards Today's Auriculas

In Victorian times in England, although the auricula was chiefly a flower of the working man, it was also grown by those with leisure at their disposal – well-off tradesmen who employed their own gardeners and a number of country parsons whose duties allowed such pursuits.

One such was the Rev. Francis Daltry Horner (1837–1912) who had a large garden at Burton in Yorkshire. His favourite flower was the auricula and his pleasure was to raise new varieties that he would often pass to a friend, Ben Simonite (1834–1909), to market. Simonite, who was a cutler, is another great name in the annals of auricula history. He repaid the compliment by naming one of his own seedlings 'The Rev F.D. Horner'. He also bred the lovely red Self, 'Fanny Meerbeck', which is still growing well today. A visit to Sheffield cemetery reveals Ben Simonite's gravestone decorated with the carving of an auricula – he was faithful to his beloved flowers even in death.

Although the Rev. Horner had a slight speech defect, nevertheless, accustomed perhaps to preaching to his flock, he did much to promote the auricula by giving talks. He also published a number of articles including a series entitled 'The Auricula' which appeared in *The Florist and Pomologist* in 1877. He was a kind, thoughtful man who tended his parishioners with as much devotion as he lavished on his plants – it is said that he travelled far to be at the bedside of a dying weaver-florist.

The Rev. Horner is also remembered as instrumental in launching the National Auricula and Primula Society which eventually split into three sections: Northern, Southern and Midland & West. A National Auricula Show was held on 24 April 1877 at Crystal Palace, at which over 1,000 plants including some excellent new seedlings were shown. It was reported as being 'the grandest display of these interesting, old-fashioned flowers which has ever been held in London or elsewhere'. The Rev. Horner left a delightful account of the auricula at this event. 'A warm and brilliant reception awaited it from far and near, from town and country, from lowly frame and cosy house. It came in its primrose modesty, from the cool shade of its violet-like seclusion, to be a noted visitor in the gay London floral season, a fresh and artless pretty country cousin ... to those who had known the Auricula long but not seen it for a weary while it was a dear old face, but little damaged by time, while to strangers it was a flower of bewildering beauty.' Many great old auriculas, some over fifty years old were shown that day: 'Pages Champion', 'Lovely Ann', 'Colonel Taylor', 'Lancashire Hero Metropolitan', 'Duke of Argyll'. The Premier flower was, of course, the relatively young 'George Lightbody'.

Membership of the societies grew. In 1881 in the Southern section there were forty-nine members who paid an annual five shillings. Throughout this time James Douglas, Charles Turner, Rev. Horner and Ben Simonite were very actively involved in exhibiting.

Not everyone was beguiled by florists' flowers. William Robinson, advocate of the natural gardening style, said in his best selling book of 1833, *The English Flower Garden* that the classification of the Show Auricula 'merely tends to throw obstacles in the way of general growth and enjoyment of the flower in the garden', adding that

Facing page: Kercup.

April Moon.

the 'curious development of the powdery matter, green margins &c tend to enfeeble the plant. They are in fact, variations that in Nature would have little or no chance of survival'. He did however, approve of Border auriculas.

Florists of course, continued to improve their plants. Edges were still regarded as the hybridizers' triumph, and Fancies were beginning to be seen at shows – although Horner had mixed feelings, referring to them as 'pale ghosts of aniline dyes; the shades of weak mustard; phantom tints of pickled cucumber'.

ALPINES COME IN FROM THE COLD

Another poorly regarded group was Alpines which, in spite of their predominance on the continent, had never really caught on to the same extent in England. Robert Sweet in *The Florists' Guide* 1827, had illustrated one, 'Howe's Venus' which he referred to as 'from a tribe called the Shaded Alpines by the Florists; they are very pretty and make an agreeable contrast with the other tribes but are not so much esteemed by the generality of Florists'. Sweet adds that the auricula in the image is from the collection of Mr Hogg of Paddington.

In fact, it even took some time for the name Alpine to be formalized. The term had apparently first been used in 1820 when a class was included at the Leeds Horticultural Show, and in the minute books of the Ancient Society of York

Florists there is an entry for 1824 referring to a class of 'shaded selfs or alpine auriculas'. These new introductions included plants called 'Alpine King', 'Alpine Queen' and 'Alpine Beauty'. In 1828 Thomas Hogg was selling Alpines at a similar price to most other sorts apart from the favoured Green Edges. In *The Gardeners' Magazine* show reports indicate that Alpines were seen more frequently at Horticultural rather than Florists' Shows. Under 'Advice to Young Florists' however, the writer said of Alpines, 'although some of them are beautifully shaded and very pretty, yet I do not think them worth the prices asked for them. Your best way would be to sow a packet of good fresh seed. I have this season seeded a whole bed of alpines'.

By 1855 another correspondent was writing, 'In the alpines there has been no improvement for many years. 'Fair Rosamund', shaded crimson is still the best; 'Conspicua', shaded blue; 'Queen Victoria' nearly black with scarlet, and a few others … ' This article also mentions the belief that it is impossible to raise good Edges where Alpines are grown. This prejudice was apparently one of the reasons why old florists wanted nothing to do with Alpines. Emmerton had grown a couple, 'Favourite' and 'Lady Sarah', which stayed the course for a few decades.

In the 1870s, the Paris firm of Vilmorin raised a new type of Alpine known as the Laced or Edged Alpine which was subsequently introduced into England by Mr A. Dean of Middlesex. A correspondent wrote to *The Garden* in April 1877 commenting that this type had 'the quiet grace and elegance of the true edged auricula without any of the staring, self asserting look which I so much dislike in the true Alpine'. He described several seedlings he had raised including 'a clear lemon centre surrounded with a ground of heavy maroon, broadly laced with a margin of pale peach'. He makes the point that in all cases three distinct tints are involved. The type met with sufficient favour to be accorded classes, and another *Garden* correspondent, the Rev. Frederick Tymons, commented that if a few faults were rectified, 'I make

Facing page: C. G. Haysom.

no doubt whatever that a brilliant future is in store for this class of plant. I would gladly grow a collection of them, while I would not admit an Alpine'. Their novelty was in fact to some extent responsible for the ordinary Alpine or Pure falling out of popularity for a while. An image of two of these appears in *The Florist and Pomologist* of 1880, but by about 1912 they had become obsolete.

As the nineteenth century came to an end, the denigrated Alpine was about to receive a boost. Charles Turner, a grower from Slough, remembered also for the introduction of the Cox's Orange Pippin apple, selected from the best available Alpines at the time and after several years' patient work, had a good list. In 1898 for the first time a gold-centred Alpine, 'Mrs Martin R. Smith' was selected for the Premier Alpine award at the NAPS Southern Section Show.

THE HOUSE OF DOUGLAS

Some of Turner's auriculas were featured on the list of another extremely important name in British auricula history, James Douglas (1837–1911). James established the House of Douglas in 1893, and three generations of his family continued to grow florist's flowers, including auriculas, in their nursery at Great Bookham, Surrey.

James Douglas was born near Kelso in Scotland and loving flowers from a very early age, he learned a lot by working in his mother's garden. His parents would have liked him to become a minister or teacher but at fourteen he insisted on going to work in a local nursery. It was there he first saw edged auriculas and was immediately smitten. In 1854 he began working in various gardens, acquiring a great deal of knowledge including something of hybridizing, before moving south to work at James Veitch's Royal Exotic Nursery at Chelsea, where he was soon helping at RHS Shows.

A little later he went back to private gardens working for a Mr Whitbourn in Essex. It was there that he raised his family of five children. He continued to play a role in RHS activities and began to contribute articles to horticultural magazines, some of which formed a basis for a book, *Hardy Florists' Flowers* published in 1879, which included a section on auriculas and was dedicated to Charles Turner. After the death of his employer in 1893 Douglas bought a parcel of land, Edenside, at Great Bookham with the intention of running his own nursery.

The first catalogue, which contained a note that he had won more prizes for auriculas than any breeder, contained seven Green Edges, seventeen Grey Edges, sixteen White Edges, fourteen Selfs and twenty-seven Alpines. This is of interest because from it we see that Edges were still top of the tree, but that Alpines, thanks probably to Turner, were now doing well. Stripes and Doubles had completely disappeared.

In the nursery, as well as plants, tweezers, pins and other sundries for their care were sold, and in fact, Douglas himself apparently used an old teapot in order to water his auriculas carefully. He was also generous with his advice and did a lot to introduce the younger generation to the delights of the fancy. One of his ways of so doing was to offer members of the southern NAPS free packets of high quality seed.

After the Boer War, in which one of his sons was killed, James was joined by his other son, James Junior (yet another father-son duo of similarly-named nurserymen!). His father continued to work at the nursery until he died in 1911. Amongst the tributes paid to him was the purchase, in his memory, of the James Douglas Memorial Cup by the NAPS Southern section, to be competed for at the annual show. It is fitting that in 2010 this section's annual show itself moved to Great Bookham.

In 1912 the Rev. Horner died and the same year James Douglas the Younger brought out his first catalogue, which contained a picture of the Alpine 'Phyllis Douglas', still available today, which he had raised in 1909. The First World War brought in its wake problems, shortages of labour and increased costs, but James struggled through it without ceasing his hybridizing. In 1930, a late season enabled him to show 'a magnificent collection' at the Chelsea Show.

The NAPS Northern section continued throughout the war and had a Victory Show in 1919, but between the two wars its membership fell and by

1932 there was only £12.00 in the bank. During the Second World War most of their activities ceased after the venue for the 1941 Show was destroyed by enemy action.

Membership of the NAPS Southern also fell. In 1921 it was only thirty-five, and by 1925 the society's cash balance reached the all-time low of 9 shillings and 3 pence. For NAPS Midland & West things were even worse. This had previously been a buoyant and enthusiastic society whose shows often ended with an evening concert party with opera singers, quartets and on one occasion a banjoist. Possibly they overspent on entertainment, for by 1930 the society folded.

In 1930 James's son Gordon joined the House of Douglas. He was particularly fond of auriculas and in the 1930s he raised 'White Wings', another plant which is still doing well today. In spite of the increased membership, it was nevertheless a lean time. Gordon gave a lecture on auriculas to the RHS in 1934 in which he noted that no book or pamphlet on the florists' auricula had been published for over fifty years. He also discussed the likelihood of the auricula's having evolved from *Primula pubescens*.

By the time the 1935 catalogue was printed only twenty Edges and Selfs and thirty-five Alpines were listed. The nursery however did continue to show at Chelsea where it initiated the fashion for using a black velvet cloth as a background for auriculas – a feature that Brenda Hyatt maintained in her displays.

NAPS Midland & West re-formed in 1938. Enthusiasts had been growing auriculas all the while and were keen to show even without prize money. The day of the first Show was rainy and one of the officers, S.E. Williams (who remained a member for fifty-nine years) was too ill to attend, but he persuaded his wife to take his entries, carrying them on the train and tram in two baskets. This she did, getting soaked in the process. He though, gained Premier for his gold-centred Alpine, 'Jenny Lind'.

Lean Days

During the Second World War much of the Douglas nursery was taken over for food production, and Gordon Douglas himself went to fight, was wounded and received the Military Cross. It was an extremely low point for the auricula. Stocks were very poor, and two wars had concentrated the minds of growers on more practical plants. Membership of the flower societies fell, and some nurseries went out of business.

The House of Douglas remained operative and continued to show plants until 1967, when the nursery was compulsorily purchased by the local council in order to build a housing estate. Gordon Douglas sold much of the stock but was loath to dispose of his 'true loves', the auriculas. These he continued to raise and sell from his own house until 1985, when he retired and entrusted his collection to Brenda Hyatt, who had a small nursery at Chatham in Kent. In 1994 she was awarded the Veitch Medal for her work with auriculas. She died in 2001.

The House of Douglas was perhaps the biggest and best but certainly not the only nursery producing auriculas in the early part of the twentieth century. J.R. Loake and Captain Hearne were successful Midland growers. Cyril Haysom originally worked as manager for G.H. Dalrymple at the Bartley Nursery in Hampshire, the auricula collection of which he eventually took over. He is commemorated in the grey edged auricula 'C.G. Haysom', raised by J.R. Loake in 1962 from a seedling of 'George Rudd'. By this time the price for an Alpine was half a crown (±£2.00) while the Show varieties ranged from half a guinea (±£8.00) upwards.

They were lean days.

Biffen, writing in 1949 had closed on an elegiac note: 'Surely however badly things may go there will always be many who find their happiness in contemplating the mysterious haunting beauty of this the most perfect of all the flowers which human efforts have brought to existence.'

Roy Genders writing nine years later echoed this sentiment. 'Perhaps the advent of automation in industry will provide greater leisure for the culture of this interesting plant and once again will auricula lovers reveal their inherent skills as growers.'

In fact there was no need for despair. Had they but known it, auriculas of an unimagined quality would be bred over the next fifty years and growers would find an abundance of the happiness to which Biffen referred.

GIFTED GROWERS CARRY ON THE GOOD WORK

If the first half of the twentieth century saw the auricula at its lowest ebb, the work done as the century progressed was crucial in reinstating the auricula as a classical florist's flower. The first wave of people involved included the Rev. C. Oscar Moreton, who in the 1850s raised a blue Self, 'Bloxham Blue' and a series of blue seedlings which were apparently beautiful but constitutionally weak and did not last. (The perfect blue auricula remains still something of a Holy Grail for auricula growers.) Fred Buckley, Jack Ballard (both past editors of the successful M&W Yearbook *Argus*), Dr Robert Newton, Derek Telford and Peter Ward all concentrated on Edges and Selfs, and Derek Telford and Arthur Delbridge worked with Alpines. They are amongst the great names of the early modern period, and many of the auriculas bred by then are still available to confirm it. Whether modern technology resulted in increased leisure or not, this and the next generation of growers were gifted with exceptional dedication and skill.

It is worth noting *en passant* that 1967 was when 'George Lightbody', then 110 years old, made his last show appearance. Today's oldest auriculas are the Alpine 'Argus' raised by J.J. Keen which dates from around 1887 and is still in fine fettle, and Ben Simonite's red Self 'Fanny Meerbeck' from 1898 which is still bright and robust. Sometimes one encounters variations in these dates depending on whether the date of raising or the date of first being benched is quoted. Names, however cannot always be relied upon; the specimens of 'Colonel Champney', which are still available are not thought to be the same as the original raised by W. Turner in 1867, and today's 'Lord Saye en Sele' is certainly not the same plant as was featured on the Kilruddery list of the Earl of Meath in 1730.

By the second half of the twentieth century, a legion of magnificent new auriculas began to come over the horizon. Stripes which were completely extinct, and Doubles which had almost disappeared, were brought back to life by the patient work of some of our hybridizing geniuses. The small but devoted band were still doing what florists had done for centuries, improving their plants. This time however they were doing so with the benefit of better growing systems and increased knowledge of plant genetics.

These were private individuals rather than professional nurserymen, for something of a separation had taken place between grower and seller. It has became more usual for the breeder to produce and show his new plants after which, sufficient stocks having built up, he makes them available to the specialist nurseries which stock auriculas.

The revival of Doubles in Britain was a big landmark. They owed their origins to plants from the United States in which as we have seen, the genetic potential for doubling had been spotted by American hybridizers. In Britain Ken Gould and a handful of other enthusiasts including Gwen Baker and Alan Hawkes persisted with the project and during the 1970s a Doubles class was added to the show schedules and the standards were redefined to include them. The work was continued by such raisers as Hazel Wood and Ed Picken and now Doubles are to be found not only in variety of sumptuous colours but also striped.

The revival of Stripes is an even more successful story as none had been seen for over a hundred years. Biffen did make an attempt to revive them using Alpines and Selfs but only obtained a few 'ragamuffins' which he considered 'interesting as curiosities' . He was not impressed and found it, 'difficult to appreciate why old-world growers were enthusiastic enough to pay almost fabulous sums for them'. The late Allan Hawkes had no such qualms. Inspired by Biffen's efforts and Ehret's 1744 painting of *The Glory of Chilton* with its black stripes and yellow background, he initiated a breeding programme in the 1960s as 'a perverse desire to disregard a topical challenge and pick up threads from the past.' His starting point was 'the gift of a red and green Fancy seedling from Dr Cecil Jones which had shown some tendency to striping.' Pollen went on to it from a normal Grey Edge and seedlings were produced 'and a nasty looking lot of mongrels they were' as Allan said. He continued for several years until 'eventually there came a tray of seedlings which could be looked at without over much wincing'. The real turning point came when he was given a Fancy called 'Conservative' by David Hadfield which occasionally appeared striped. By using this plant he obtained vastly improved seedlings. Pollen from Allan Guest's best seedlings also played a role.

'Marion Tiger', a red with white and grey mealy stripes was one of his great achievements because it overcame a fault common to many Stripes, crimpy or 'nibbled' edges. These occur because of the difference of tissue texture of the striped part, caused as Biffen suggests, because the meal of the stripe inhibits the growth of the tissue beneath it. Allan Hawkes spent ten years recreating Stripes and in the late 1980s he wrote an article in *Argus* inviting others to help. Derek Parsons responded with the result that the project continued and Allan lived to see Stripes accepted, enjoyed and with classes of their own.

Derek Salt, who was also working on Stripes produced some Striped Doubles in tandem with his Singles. His Lincoln series is an amazing group of plants, unusual both in their form and the range of never-before-seen, greenery-yallery colours which they manifest. Allan Guest's 'Brimstone and Treacle' is another oddly-coloured (the name says it all) but fascinating, Striped Double.

It is Derek Parsons however, who took up the baton from Allan Hawkes, who now breeds quantities of delectable Stripes of a quality that would amaze and delight the collectors of the past. All his plants are line-bred with nothing being brought in from outside. By painstaking selection of only the most vigorous of seedlings, he has produced a wide range of colour combinations and improved forms. It is difficult to choose from his galaxy of stars but one of the most popular is 'Night and Day', which is has a delicate bluish lavender-coloured ground evenly striped with white meal.

THE NAMING GAME

All serious raisers have the task (which, from having bred dogs I know is fun at first, but less so as time goes by) of selecting names for their seedlings. Many use names of family members, for what is more delightful than to be commemorated by a flower? Allan Hawkes was a devotee of vintage bicycles, which provided a theme, and thus we find 'Raleigh Stripe' and 'Singer Stripe'. Derek Parsons however, loves the songs of Cole Porter and Frank Sinatra, so we encounter a number of very romantic names amongst his raisings. Care is needed however – having named one auricula after the Frank Sinatra song 'Take Me', he was more than a little miffed to return to the show bench on one occasion and find that someone had …

Such is the esteem of Stripes that they currently enjoy numerous classes on the show bench, and a National Collection has now been established. They are also widely distributed with around a hundred cultivars available in commerce.

It is significant that the name of one plant crops up quite often when the renaissance of Stripes is mentioned – 'Mrs Dargan'. Although now very ancient and rare, this old Fancy still just about survives. With a mix of deepish red and whitish-yellow striping sometimes, but not always, with some doubling of the petals, it cannot be said to be the most stunning of auriculas – indeed Allan Hawkes wrote that she 'has almost every imaginable fault' and continued, 'even if classed as a Border it would be considered rough'. Both Allan and Derek did use Mrs Dargan in early breeding but said they regretted it. Nevertheless, one of the most important roles the old lady played was as a reminder that stripes were *possible*.

Today the decorative qualities of the auricula are no less inspiring to artists. Eliot Hodgkin painted a series, somewhat reminiscent of Furber, called *Twelve Months of the Year,* in which auriculas are featured in the month of April. These small detailed works, in the tricky medium of tempera on board, result in wonderful luminosity of colour.

The velvety texture of the flowers also makes them a perfect subject for painting on vellum, a surface which enhances their brilliant jewel-like colours. This was exhibited by Nicholas Robert and Alexander Marshall in the past, but a skilled artist working in more recent times in this medium was Rory McEwan (1932–82) great-great grandson of John Lindley of the RHS library. His striking paintings of auriculas have inspired many contemporary botanical artists, and his influence along with the notable painter Jenny Brasier has been instrumental in reviving the use of vellum. Several of his auricula plates were reproduced to illustrate C. Oscar Moreton's book *The Auricula*, which is now out of print.

Designers too still succumb to their charms. Kaffe Fasset designed a fabric showing dozens of auricula pips in various colours. Osborne and Little produced a popular curtain fabric depicting auriculas, and they are the subject of numerous tapestry cushions – and as in the seventeenth century they still provide exquisite patterns for embroidery. Wedgewood and Queens are but two of the many factories which have produced china and porcelain decorated with auriculas, and Emma Bridgewater in 2010 added auriculas to the popular pottery range called Botany, which she produces in tandem with the National Gardens Scheme.

NO AURICULA CAN LIVE FOR EVER

A development experienced by real auriculas in the 1980s was micropropagation. Known as meristem or tissue culture, this consists of taking a tiny piece of plant material and causing it to multiply rapidly under laboratory conditions. The large number of plantlets thus produced can then be grown on for sale. This does address the imbalance between supply and demand, especially in the case of auriculas that produce few offsets or of ancient plants which have become very rare.

The technology has always been controversial as sometimes the microprogated plants did not come true. Further many people disagreed with the whole concept. Dr Frank Taylor of Wye College worked on this process for some years and did certainly bring some old and venerable varieties back from the brink of extinction. He, however,

monitored the experiments thoroughly and only dealt in small numbers.

Attractive as the idea of conserving these old varieties is, ultimately we have to recognize that no auricula can live for ever – unless, that is, science comes up with a way of giving plants eternal life, which might seem impossible, just as micropropagation would have seemed impossible to the Bobarts, Rae or Emmerton. And would it be desirable? During one of my interesting conversations with Derek Parsons, new insights into certain aspects of plant vigour were brought home to me. Derek, whose eyes look to the future rather than the past, pointed out that it is only by growing from seed that the potential of new auriculas can be realized. Even an offset contains the same genetic material as its parent plant, and if that parent plant is old and worn out, so is the offset. Seed, Derek claims, regenerates, introducing new variability and vigour from the gene pool to take the auricula further.

What more is there to do?

Reviving the Painted Lady

As we have seen there is interest in reviving the Painted Lady, and it was claimed by Brian Coop writing in *Argus* 2004 that it has already made an appearance. He cites auriculas in Derek Parson's breeding programme on which a covering of farina all over the pip overlays two or more colours, adding 'the problem is deciding whether the farina adds to the beauty of the multi-coloured striping or mutes it too much.'

In fact as we have seen Derek Parsons recognizes two sorts of farina, an opaque sort and a translucent almost crystalline sort. Derek further believes that Stripes should be made up of permanent striping and not simply composed of the thick farina which could be wiped away. In the case of Painted Ladies the consensus is that they were heavily mealed as in Derek's 'Seeing a Ghost'. This mealing in fact, Derek considers a disadvantage. He thinks the potential Painted Lady might be 'messy and difficult to bring to the show bench'.

Facing page: Dusky Maiden.

This however will not prevent others like Maedythe Martin in Canada from attempting to revive what was once considered the most perfect form of the Show Auricula. This attempt will almost certainly be successful. Brian Coop posed the further question 'How will we recognize it when we have got there?' and comments that they are unlikely to be the same as the Painted Ladies of old. Fashion may come around but it never quite repeats itself.

We shall have to wait and see.

The Fancy

Nothing in horticulture is static. Derek Parsons considers that perhaps the biggest development to have taken place is the redefinition of the Fancy. Traditionally the Fancy tended to be an inferior version of the Edge, basically a plant of any body colour other than black, although other types which could not be fitted into the established categories often began their lives there – as indeed the Stripe did.

In earlier centuries Edges could be of any body colour, indeed we have read of glorious violet-bodied Edges in at the time of Emmerton. A little later however, the Victorians decided to limit this body colour to black. In his book Allan Guest mentions an intriguing notion that the rise of the black body colour around the mid-nineteenth century reflected the general state of mourning after the death of Prince Albert – he does, however, add that a more likely explanation is that black was simply favoured as more striking and solid than weaker body colours.

Currently however, the position has been reversed, as it was decided in the 1990s that Edges can once more be of any body colour. This, to some extent leaves a void in the Fancy Class and so attention has now been diverted into developing new, interesting and beautiful Show Auriculas, which can at least start their lives amongst the Fancies.

The Shaded Self

It is here we find another interesting emergent type, the Clouded or Shaded Self. This sounds like a contradiction in terms, as in the normal Show Self no suspicion of shading is allowed. These newcomers however, are plants in which the ring of paste is surrounded by petals in which the colour shades out towards the edges. The Rev. Horner would not have approved; writing in 1877 he said, 'the Self with its densely mealed centre, must not trespass on the shadings of the Alpine, nor the Alpine appropriate the pure ground colours of the Self. Intermixture and confusion amongst them … are to be deprecated. If there be Self Alpines, why not Alpine Selfs and a host of perplexing half-breeds?'

Today's Clouded Self is no half-breed. It is in fact a lovely thing. Allan Guest illustrates one, Henry Pugh's 'Little Amber', which shades from light orange near the paste to tinted cream at the edge. One of the key plants involved in this development was a charming novelty, a Fancy called 'Moon Fairy' bred by Cliff Timpson, which has most of the attributes of a good Show Auricula. In this flower the colour beyond the ring of paste begins a pale cream but becomes suffused with a pinky violet as it reaches the edge of the petal. This is still being used in some hybridizing programmes.

Derek Parsons has produced a quantity of exquisitely coloured Clouded Self seedlings, but in his case the break came about spontaneously from open pollination of his Stripes, and indeed in some the seedlings the shading does take the form of a smudged stripe. At the moment there is no consensus as to whether this will eventually constitute a new type or whether it is simply an odd deviation, but having seen the seedlings in question I cannot but hope that it will become established and accepted.

The Laced or Edged Alpine

Florists now, as always, are searching for better colour combinations and more interesting forms, and another category on which at least one hybridizer is working is a revival of the Laced or Edged Alpine. This developed from the Luiker or Alpine type from the continent and is an Alpine in which

Facing page: Raleigh Stripe Seedling.

instead of the gradual shading from dark to light in the body colour the transition is sudden and a distinct rim of colour is visible, as in the laced polyanthus.

Les Allen initiated the revival. Writing in *Argus* in 1998 he describes finding a plant of 'Vulcan' in which one of the seven pips showed distinct signs of lacing. He cut off the other pips and pollinated the remaining one with 'Frank Crossland'. He then crossed the progeny of this union with an unnamed seedling which also showed a tendency to lacing, and of the sixty seedlings he selected three, one of which showed shading and lacing.

He continues to breed along these lines and at the time of writing, 2010, has three cultivars which are close to the standard he set out to achieve. The only one to have been shown – and so named (Les Allen follows the tradition of only naming a seedling when it has achieved a first or second prize on the show bench) is 'Blue Lace', but the other two he hopes to bench next year. His colour range in the Light Centres now includes some pink, and he has a strain of Gold Centres which also look promising. Such is the patience required for this work that, he told me, 'from some 100 plants I have selected two that look worthwhile continuing with' and these he has used as this year's seed parents. Classes were instigated for this category at the NAPS Midland and West Shows, the auricula 'Pequod' being twice a winner, but the entries were sparse. The Southern and Northern sections have yet to accept this type, so once again we shall have to wait to see if this becomes an acceptable variation.

Thus it is apparent that the story is not over yet.

Having followed the Bear's Ear down from the high Alps and into the collections of the curious across Europe, having seen it arrive in London gardens to the delight of Gerard and Parkinson while at the same time going on to embellish the gardens of princely estates on the continent, having toasted its beauty at feasts in the company of florists, having watched weavers and miners growing outstanding specimens in cramped conditions and having seen today's outstanding auriculas on the show bench – we can sense from the amazing potential of this tiny flower that the journey is still ongoing. In 1877 the Rev. Horner wrote, 'there is nothing to prove to us that we have in any of our florists-flowers reached motionless perfection yet.'

Wonderful auriculas are yet to come.

Douglas Green.

'The Gardener' from *The Book of English Trades*, 1824.

Appendix: Today's Auricula Enthusiasts

In this Appendix I have invited some of today's auricula enthusiasts to tell of their passion.

The Dowager Marchioness of Salisbury

Garden designer and president of the Garden Museum, London, whose family has had connections with auriculas for over four centuries

I began growing auriculas at Cranborne, having fallen utterly in love with them at first sight. When, after my father-in-law's death we moved to Hatfield I took the small greenhouse where I grew my stage auriculas and set it up in the place I designed a few years later in the kitchen garden. What exquisite pleasure they gave each year in the weeks of April and May when they were in flower! I joined the Auricula Society and looked forward each year to the displays at Chelsea and the Royal Horticultural Shows in London and new plants were added to my collection.

Some years later I had a small auricula theatre made and hung it in the east wall of one of the garden houses on the south front of Hatfield. It was in painted wood with a proscenium arch and side curtains. The curtains were dark green with tie backs and braided in deep yellow. The dark tobacco-brown interior was a good background to show off the trusses and the pots sat on shelves inside. I now have it fixed on a panel of the trellis which surrounds my roof garden in London.

One day, Gregory Long, President of the New York Botanical Garden visited and asked me if I would design an auricula theatre for his Botanical Garden. It was a commission after my own heart. John Tradescant, whose garden Gerard described in his *Herball*, worked at Hatfield in 1601. In 1815 Issac Emmerton dedicated his Treatise on the Culture and Management of the Auricula to one of my predecessors, the 2nd Marchioness of Salisbury. So when in 2007 I cut the ribbon to open the Auricula Theatre on that sunny day in New York, I was happy to be bringing the connection with this lovely flower into the twenty-first century.

Allan Guest

One of the leading judges and hybridizers, and author of The Auricula

I stumbled into the world of auriculas in the 1960s when I began crossing polyanthus to provide some colour under the roses. I had also just raised some seedlings from the Barnhaven range which were causing such a stir at the time. After some effort (no Internet in those days, remember), I found the National Auricula and Primula Society and went along to the shows. I was dumbfounded at the range of plants displayed there. The forms, the colours and the scents were scarcely credible. After a few attempts on the show bench with old and none too shapely plants, newer ones were offered to me free or at a moderate cost in the sales for Society members only. The itch to present them at their very best (and always with that challenge of doing it just that bit better than anyone else) and also of using them to create even more beautiful variations on the theme has never gone away.

When individuals comment that they do not see the attraction of the auricula, it is always interesting to discover their tastes in music, literature or painting. For me, there is much of the precise beauty and economy of the string quartet (or of wonderful creations such as T.S. Eliot's literary variations from the same genre) in the form and balance of a well-grown and skilfully presented auricula. Their range of colour and form, with its nostalgia for what has gone before and its promise of what may still be developed, recall Brahms's symphonic creations.

Ina ten Hove-Janesma

Dutch correspondent of the author, who works to promote the auricula

I'm a novice collector from The Netherlands. Twelve years ago I read an article about the Auricula in a Dutch garden magazine. At that time nurseries introduced a 'plant of the month', and that month their highlight was the *Primula auricula* 'Hawkwood'. I was an enthusiastic gardener and never heard about that plant. I went to the library, and my interest was awakened when I read that the Auricula had such a history in my country. Why didn't I know that before?

Then I made a garden trip to the Talbot Garden of Malahide in Dublin and saw a little Victorian greenhouse of flowering auriculas. I was overwhelmed with the glory of their colours and their smell. I wanted that at home too! In the meantime I had bought the *Hawkwood* from a Dutch nursery but then it closed and as I wanted more plants I had to buy from abroad. So I thought, why not in the UK? Then I got membership of the NAPS and all the information I needed.

My contacts with other enthusiasts from Scandinavia, Germany, Belgium, Japan, New Zealand, Ireland and of course the UK are important to me. We learn from each other and swap our off-shoots. I've got now about 250 different varieties. The Auricula is also well worth re-discovering in my own country so for the last year I've been busy with lectures, exhibitions at local markets and publishing article.

Andy Kemp

Our modern Florist of Bath, a very successful exhibitor

When I saw my first picture of an auricula, the precision of the zones and clarity of colours had

me hooked. I now grow a collection of all the classes of florists' auriculas for the purpose of exhibiting. For me there is an excitement in competing with others, but the real thrill comes when you see the look on the faces of newcomers to the shows as they view these fascinating plants for the first time.

As one of the younger growers, it falls to me to look to the future. The commonly perceived threats are from climate change and the spread of new pests and diseases; fashion also can also be fatal for plants. However due to the diversity and hardy nature of these flowers, they would appear to have staying power. Auriculas make the perfect hobby plant because they are easy to grow, but hard to grow well. The striving for perfection requires discipline and judgment, qualities that will stand anyone well in their day-to-day lives. Even though the pips fade in a matter of weeks, for those who love auriculas there is year-round interest.

So how have the modern growers done with the challenges set by their floral forefathers? I do not think that the perfect plant will ever exist, except perhaps in the mind of the florist at that moment when they dap pollen on pin and dream of the potential of the progeny. This does raise the question 'what is the point of striving for perfection, when perfection cannot be achieved?' Perhaps the answer is that it is not always about the destination, but the journey.

Maedythe Martin

A Canadian hybridizer and enthusiastic promoter of auriculas in the New World

It all began with a velvety-purple garden auricula that caught my eye at a local garden club plant stall in the 1970s. I was working and had a two-year-old: gardening time was limited. Although it took a decade, I did master growing auriculas. Sadly, many of the early ones I had perished in the process, but I persisted. I joined the local alpine gardening group, the American Primrose Society and NAPS Southern to learn more.

Showing auriculas at the alpine group's spring show, I met Cy Happy, a long-time member of the APS from Washington State. He came up to Victoria each year to judge the *Primula* classes, and began to give me plants and also taught me how to pollinate auriculas.

In 1996 I was able, for the first time in eighteen years, to visit England, specifically to hear Allan Hawkes talk on striped auriculas. I'd inhaled any mention of these in the NAPS yearbooks and become entranced by them. Allan was very kind and encouraging and became a great friend. On subsequent visits to England I met other kind mentors: Derek Salt, Derek Parsons and Geoff Nicolle.

I began crossing the plants I had, and despite odd first-generation flowers, I now have some presentable stripes. My next goal is to develop striped doubles and the old 'Painted Ladies' with meal all over their faces. Being so far from a source of auricula plants, I find growing from seed is the answer. And once you start hybridizing, you can have lots.

Derek Parsons

A leading hybridizer and raiser of those fabulous Stripes

Hay-on-Wye is world renowned for its bookshops, but to me it will always be the place I first saw Show Auriculas 'in the flesh'. I had seen pictures of them in books and I was attracted to them, but to see them in real life was a jaw-dropping experience. Love came to me in a small nursery devoted to Alpines. Really it was a garden behind a house in an ordinary street, and I found myself in a large greenhouse filled with Show Auriculas mostly in full flower. There were Edges, Selfs and Alpines (this expertise came later after I had digested several textbooks on the auricula). I became aware of someone watching me. Apparently I had strayed into the owner's private collection, 'Not For Sale', but such is the generous nature of auricula growers that half an hour later I left with a dozen gorgeous plants. Among them was a ragamuffin, a very old remnant of the Striped Auriculas 'Mrs Dargan', obviously well past her best.

To cut a long story short, for the next twenty years I ended up raising new varieties of Stripes.

After the first few years I took my best, but still only half-decent, seedlings to a National Show. Since no one else was growing Stripes at this time I did quite well, but I can still see those grubby, square, black pots that I used. Tim Coop, a legend in the auricula world, took me to one side and explained a few things about Show etiquette but gently added, 'Still, you must be doing something right.' I positively glowed.

For me, auriculas are the bedrock of my retired life. If you let them they will lead you into history, photography, computers, giving slide shows and making friends. They satisfy the needs of the collector, the showman, the perfectionist, the hybridist, the artist and the romantic. Perhaps the greatest pleasure comes in the spring when the previous year's pollinations flower for the first time and promise us continuing joy. Pure magic!

Brigitte Wachsmuth

A German plant historian and author of Die Aurikel, *the first German monograph solely on the auricula since 1783*

When the philosopher Immanuel Kant was asked what he would recommend for distinguished male apparel he advised the following, 'a brown jacket fits a yellow waistcoat – this teaches us about the auricula.'

What makes the auricula unique in the empire of garden plants is the fact that its refined beauty is as delectable aesthetically as its special history is intellectually. All the dedicated breeders, aristocratic devotees, cunning plant merchants, curious naturalists and accomplished flower painters, the French *fleuristes*, the Flemish *bloemisten*, the German *aurikulisten* and above all, the English florists have made the auricula a plant beyond comparison.

There are many precious jewels from the past. Indiana Jones' famous quote 'that belongs in a museum' luckily does not fit this one; it is still living and thriving in our gardens.

In his essay on education Kant draws another analogy between the successful upbringing of children and the breeding of auriculas, regarding the development of desirable characteristics. He seems to have been a faithful admirer of the delicate flower. So am I.

Chris and Hazel Wood

Well-known raisers of Doubles and Show Auriculas, both truly worthy of the name 'florist'

Chris writes: We became interested in auriculas some thirty odd years ago when I noticed an interesting plant in my sister-in-law's garden, which turned out to be a Border Auricula. Eventually this led to contact with the Midland Auricula and Primula Society from where plants were subsequently obtained. Around that time, Brian Coop and Eddie Picken also joined the society; we were all of a similar age and all four of us are still members.

Now Hazel has taken up Doubles while I concentrate on Show Auriculas and Gold Laced Polyanthus. We are particularly interested in breeding plants to a high standard, and Hazel has been successful in exhibiting many winning Double seedlings. An early success was 'Mipsie Miranda' in 1982, and latterly 'Daisy Wood' a white Double seedling went Best in Show at the Midland Show. I have produced several promising Green and Grey Edged seedlings but am still in search of the outstanding plant. At the present time I am also breeding a few Blue Self Show Auriculas.

Our main aim is to breed plants that are worthy of the ideals set by the pioneers of the auricula, which are beautiful in their own right and as near to the standard of perfection as possible.

Susan Dickinson

Head Gardener to Lord Rothschild at Eythrope

The Eythrope Auricula collection began as a gift of two hundred plants from a gardening friend who was winding down her collection. Lord Rothschild felt they needed to be displayed so their beauty could be admired. An Auricula Theatre was built of oak in the north-east corner of the Eythrope walled garden. The plants are also used to decorate the house on a circular glass staging placed on a marble table. We grow the plants in clay pots in a shady Alpine House, and find the Society Shows a good source of new plants.

Bibliography

Arber, Agnes, *Herbals* (Cambridge University Press, 1938)

Baker, Gwen and Peter Ward, *Auriculas* (Batsford, 1995)

Barker, Nicolas, *Hortus Eystettensis* (The British Library, 1994)

Bauhin, Caspar, *Pinax Theatrum Botannicum* (1617)

Biffen, Sir Rowland, *The Auricula* (London, 1949)

Blacker, Mary Rose, *Flora Domestica* (National Trust, 2000)

Blunt, Wilfred, *Tulipomania* (Penguin, 1950)

Buc'hoz, Pierre Joseph, *La Toilette de Flore* (1784)

Bradley, Richard, *New Improvements of Planting and Gardening* (1731)

Clark, Timothy, *Mary McMurtrie's Country Garden Flowers* (Garden Art Press, 2009)

Clusius, Carolus, *Rariorum aliquot stirpium per Pannoniam, Austriam & vicinis* (Antwerp, 1583)

Clusius, Carolus, *Rariorum plantarum Historia* (Antwerp, 1601)

Coats, Alice, *Flowers and Their Histories* (Adam & Charles Black, 1968)

Cotteret, Bernard, *Huguenots in England* (University of Cambridge, 1991)

Cottesloe, Gloria and Doris Hunt, *The Duchess of Beaufort's Flowers* (Webb & Bower, 1983)

Defoe, Daniel, *The Complete English Tradesman* (1726)

Dodoens, Rembert, *Herbal* (1619)

Donzel, Catherine, *The Book of Flowers* (Flammarion, 1998)

Duthie, Ruth, *Florists' Flowers & Societies* (Aylesbury, 1988)

Egmond, Florike (ed.), *Clusius: Towards a Cultural History of a Renaissance Naturalist* (2007)

Emmerton, Issac, *A Plain and Practical Treatise on the Culture and Management of the Auricula* (1815)

Ferrari, Giovanni Battista, *Flora seu de Florum Cultura* (1646)

Findlen, Paula, *Possessing Nature, Museums, Collecting and Scientific Culture* (University of California, 1996)

Franeau, Jean, *Le Jardin d'Hyver* (1616)

Furber, Robert, *Twelve Months of Flowers* (1730)

Furber, Robert, *The Flower Garden Displayed* (1732)

Genders, Roy, *Auriculas* (London, 1958)

Gerard, John, *Herball*, London, 1597)

Gerard, John, *Herball*, edited by Thomas Johnson (London, 1633)

Gesner, Conrad, *Opera Botanica* (1751)

Gilbert, Samuel, *The Florists Vade-Mecum* (1682)

Gilmour, John, *British Botanists* (Collins, 1956)

Goldgar, Anne, *Tulipmania* (University of Chicago, 2007)

Guest, Allan, *The Auricula* (Garden Art Press, 2009)

Guénin, Charles, *Traité de la Culture des Oreilles d'Ours* (Paris, 1735)

Hadfield, Miles, *A History of British Gardening* (Penguin, 1985)

Hanbury, William, *A Complete Body of Plants and Gardening* (1770)

Hanmer, Sir Thomas, *The Garden Book*, with introduction by Eleanour Sinclair Rohde (Clwyd, 1933)

Harris, Walter, *A Description of the King's Royal Palace and Gardens at Loo* (1699)

Harwood, Catherine, *Potted History* (Frances Lincoln, 2007)

Hecker, W.R., *Auriculas and Primroses* (Batsford, 1971)

Hogg, Thomas, *A Concise and Practical Treatise* (1820)

Hyde, Elizabeth, *Cultivated Power: Flowers Culture and Politics in the Reign of Louis XIV* (University of Pennsylvania, 2005)

Jacquin, Nicolai Joseph, *Flora Austriaca* (1773)

Jefferson, Thomas, *The Garden Book* (1767)

Justice, James, *British Gardener's Directory* (1769)

Kannegiesser, *Aurikel Flora nach der Natur gemahlt* (1801)

La Chesnée Monstereul, *Le Floriste Français* (1654)

Laird, Mark, *The Flowering of the English Landscape Garden* (University of Pennsylvania, 1999)

Leith-Ross, Prudence, *The Tradescants* (London, 1984)

Loudon, John Claudius, *An Encyclopaedia of Gardening* (1835*)*

Mahood, M.M., *The Poet as Botanist* (Cambridge University, 2008)

Marshall, Alexander, *Mr Marshall's Flower Book* (Royal Collection, 2008)

Mattoli, Pier Andrea, *Opera Qua extant omnia* (1598)

Michiel, Pietro Antonio, *I Cinque Libri di Piante* (1551–75)

Miller, Philip, *The Gardener's Kalender* (1765)

Miller, Philip, *The Gardener's Dictionary* (1731)

Moet, Jean Paul, *Traité de la Culture ... des auricules* (1754)

Moreton, C. Oscar, *The Auricula* (The Ariel Press, 1964)

Morin, Pierre, *Remarques Nécessaires pour la culture des Fleurs* (1678)

Nelson, Charles E., *A Heritage of Beauty, Garden Plants of Ireland* (2000, Irish Garden Plant Society)

Parkinson, John, *Paradisus* (1629)

Parkinson, John, *Theatrum Botanicum* (1640)

Parkinson, Anna, *Nature's Alchemist* (Frances Lincoln, 2007)

Pavord, Anna, *The Tulip* (London, 1999)

Pavord, Anna, *The Naming of Names* (2005)

Rae, John, *Flora de Flora Cultura* (1665)

Robinson, Mary, *Auriculas for Everyone* (Lewes, 2001)

Rohde, Eleanour Sinclair, *The Scented Garden* (Medici Society, 1931)

Rohde, Eleanour Sinclair, *The Story of the Garden* (Medici Society, 1932/1989)

Sitwell, Sacheverell, *Old Fashioned Flowers* (London, 1939)

Sweet, Robert, *The Florist's Guide* (1827)

Sweerts, Emanuel, *Florilegium Amplissimum* (1647)

Tarver, David, *Auricula History* (NAPS Guide No.5)

Tarver, David, *Auricula Miscellany* (NAPS Guides, 1999)

Thomas, K.V., *Man and the Natural World* (Allen Lane, 1983)

Tongiorgi Tomasi, Lucia, *An Oak Spring Flora* (Oak Spring Garden Library, 1997)

Vallet, Pierre, *Le Jardin du Roy tres chrestien Henry IV Roy de France* (1608)

Valnay, *Connoissance et Culture parfaite des Belles Fleurs* (1688)

Van de Passe, Crispin *Hortus Floridus* (1614)

Van Oosten, Hendrick, *The Dutch Gardener* (1703)

Van Sprang, Sabine *L'Empire de Flore* (Brussels, 1996)

Volkammer, J.G., *Flora Noribergensis* or *Nurnbergishe Hesperides* (1700)

Wachsmuth, Brigitte and Nickig, Marion, *Die Aurikel* (Ellert & Richter, 2009)

Walsh, Wendy F., Ruth Isobel Ross and E. Charles Nelson, *An Irish florilegium; the wild and gardens flowers of Ireland* (Thames and Hudson, 1983).

Ward, Peter, *Primroses and Auriculas* (London, 2003)

White, Michelle, *Henrietta Maria and the English Civil Wars* (Fontana, 2006)

ARTICLES

Duthie, Ruth, 'English Florists' Societies and Feasts' (*Garden History*, Vol.10, No.1, 1982)

Duthie, Ruth, 'English Florists' Societies and Feasts' (*Garden History*, Vol.12, No.1, 1984)

Gould, Jim, 'James Maddock', (*Garden History*, Vol.19, No.2, 1991)

Gould, Jim, 'The Tuggies of Westminster' (*Garden History*, 1992)

Gould, Jim, 'Isaac Emmerton, Thomas Hogg and their Composts' (*Garden History*, 1989)

Hyde, Elisabeth, 'Flowers of Distinction: Taste, Class, and Floriculture in Seventeenth-Century France', in *Bourgeois and Aristocratic Encounters in the Garden,* ed. Michel Conan (Washington, D.C.: Dumbarton Oaks Research Library and Collection, 2002)

Laird, Mark and John Harvey, 'A late 18th Century Town Garden' (*Garden History*, 1997)

Nelson, Charles, 'The Dublin Flower Club' (*Garden History*, 1982)

Robinson, Jenny, 'New Light on Sir Thomas Hanmer' (*Garden History*, 1988)

Woudstra, Jan, 'The Greenhouse Quarter at Hampton Court' (*Garden History*, Vol.37, No.1, 2009)

Useful Addresses

NURSERIES SELLING AURICULAS

Angus Plants, Balfour Cottages, Menmuir,
   By Brechin, Angus DD9 7RN
   www.angusplants.co.uk

Drointon Nurseries, Plaster Pitts, Norton Conyers,
   Ripon, N. Yorks HG4 5EF
   www.auricula-plants.co.uk

Field House Nurseries, Leake House, Gotham, Notts.
   NG11 0JN
   val.wooley@btinternet.com

W & S Lockyer, 39 Mitchley Ave, Riddlesdown,
   Purley, Surrey CR8 1BZ
   Tel/Fax 0208 660 1336

Pops Plants, Barford Lane, Downton, Salisbury, Wilts.
   SP5 3PZ
   www.popsplants.co.uk

Woottens Plants, Blackheath, Wenhaston, Halesworth,
   Suffolk IP19 9HD
   www.woottensplants.co.uk

**NATIONAL AURICULA AND PRIMULA
SOCIETY**

Southern Section

Lawrence Wigley, 67, Warnham Court Road,
   Carshalton Beeches, Surrey SM5 3ND
   www.southernauriculaprimula.org

Midland & West

David Tarver, Church Street, Belton, Loughborough,
   Leics. LE12 9UG
   www.auriculaandprimula.org.uk

Northern

R. Taylor, 22 Temple Rhydding Drive, Baildon,
   Shipley, W. Yorks BD17 5PU
   www.auriculas.org.uk

Limited edition prints of the illustrations in this book
are available from www.elisabethdowle.com

Index